Tuning My Heart

Tuning My Heart

*The Melody of the Liturgical Year
in Proclamation, Poetry, and Praise*

LAURIE ANN KRAUS

WIPF & STOCK · Eugene, Oregon

TUNING MY HEART
The Melody of the Liturgical Year in Proclamation, Poetry, and Praise

Copyright © 2008 Laurie Ann Kraus. All rights reserved. Except for brief quotations in critical publications or reviews, no part of this book may be reproduced in any manner without prior written permission from the publisher. Write: Permissions, Wipf and Stock Publishers, 199 W. 8th Ave., Suite 3, Eugene, OR 97401.

www.wipfandstock.com

ISBN 13: 978-1-55635-208-9

Manufactured in the U.S.A.

Scripture taken from THE MESSAGE, Copyright © 1993, 1994, 1995, 1996, 2000, 2001, 2002. Used by permission of NavPress Publishing Group.

Scripture quotations contained herein are from The Holy Bible. Revised Standard Version, New York: Thomas Nelson and Sons, 1973 by the Division of Christian Education of the National Council of the Churches of Christ in the U.S.A., and are used by permission. All rights reserved.

Scripture quotations contained herein are from the New Revised Standard Version Bible, copyright © 1989 by the Division of Christian Education of the National Council of the Churches of Christ in the U.S.A., and are used by permission. All rights reserved.

Scripture quotations contained herein are from Coogan, Michael D., ed.. The New Oxford Annotated Bible, Third Edition, New Revised Standard Version. Oxford: Oxford University Press: 2001, and are used by permission. All rights reserved.

Scripture quotations contained herein are from Scofield, C. I., The Scofield Reference Bible: The Holy Bible, Authorized King James Version. New York: Oxford University Press, 1945, and are used by permission. All rights reserved.

Scripture quotations taken from TANAKH: The Holy Scriptures: The New JPS Translation According to the Traditional Hebrew Text, copyright © 1988. Used by permission of the Jewish Publication Society.

for Gillian and Warren
and for my parents
who keep the melody going while I sing harmony

Contents

Acknowledgments ix

1 Tuning My Heart: The Melody of the Liturgical Year in Proclamation, Poetry, and Praise 1

2 The Scent of Incarnation: Advent and Christmastide 5
    Et Incarnatus Est
    O Holy Nightmare
    The Invisible Man
    Baptizing the Bulgarians
    The Six-Toed Jesus
    After the Angels
    Birth Pangs

3 Hints of Dreams: Epiphany to Transfiguration Sunday 35
    Seeking Stars
    A Place to Begin
    Insignificant Matters
    "Something Very Basic"
    Holy Roller Coaster
    Benedictions and Beginnings
    Till We Have Faces

4 When the Lights Go Down: The Season of Lent 69
    Sacred Space
    The Wailing Wall
    The Blind Leading
    Overdone
    Baggage
    Saturday's God
    Holy Week Triptych

5 The Acts of Orchids: Easter Day to Ascension 99
   Resisting Resurrection
   The Opposite of Certainty
   The Green Flash
   Nahshon's Story
   In Over Our Heads
   Saints and Widows
   Rites of Passage
   Ascension: Acts 1

6 The Greening of the Gospel: The Festival of Pentecost Through
                Christ the King 134
   Once Upon a Time ...
   E Pluribus Unum
   Homemade Sin
   "More Immediate Concerns"
   Losing God
   Dancing With Chaos
   Cry Me a River
   An Embarrassing Anachronism

   Bibliography 175

Acknowledgments

I AM GRATEFUL FOR the stories, support, and love of the communities in which my life, faith, and vocation have unfolded. This collection would not be possible without any of them. Together and individually, their lives have composed the music to which these words are set. I thank God for you all: my families of birth and choice, the people of Riviera Presbyterian Church in Miami, and the community of learning that is the Florida Center for Theological Studies where I am privileged to teach.

You all know who you are, and what you are to me. Particular thanks to my friend, Father Patrick O'Neill, and to Riviera Presbyterian Church who offered me a sabbatical and the resources to sustain it so that I could have time and space to complete this volume; and to my friend Jim Mulder, who carefully and lovingly proofread the text before publication.

1

Tuning My Heart

The Melody of the Liturgical Year in Proclamation, Poetry, and Praise

> Come, thou fount of every blessing, tune my heart to sing thy grace
> Streams of mercy, never ceasing, call for songs of loudest praise
> Teach me some melodious sonnet, sung by flaming tongues above
> Praise the mount! I'm fixed upon it, mount of God's unchanging love.
> —"Come Thou Fount of Every Blessing,"
> Robert Robinson, 1758[1]

On All Saint's Day, 1988, with the envious farewells of my snowbound friends back in upstate New York still echoing in my mind, I stepped into the pulpit of the Miami congregation that was my new church home for the first time. Dressed professionally in a suit, heels, hosiery, and my new "three season" wool Geneva pulpit robe, sweat was pouring down my face and body before I had finished the call to worship. It was November in the sub-tropics, and between the palm trees waving outside my office window and the wild peacock screaming like a banshee from the roof of the manse in which my small family had taken up residence, I was one disoriented pastor—or, as I was fast learning to describe myself in this not-actually-the-deep south edge of the world—preacher. *Surely*, I thought, *it will be winter soon*. But it was not. November passed, then Thanksgiving. We wore shorts and ate turkey on the back patio, shaded by trees still in the full leaf of midsummer. Driving down the highway on my way to meetings or visits with new parishioners, I would look at flowers in riotous bloom and be suddenly struck by confusion—was it November, or June? When was I? December came, and with it, my daughter's second

---

1. *The Hymnbook*, Presbyterian Church in the United States of America, #379.

Christmas. The year before, we had donned parkas and boots, tromped a mile through the snow, and cut down our own tree, paying the farmer $10 for the privilege. In Miami, the temperature hovered in the mid-eighties. I waited in vain for the Christmas spirit to strike, then finally gave up and went to the grocery store to look for a tree whose needles had not yet shriveled in the heat. *Maybe,* I mused, *it would be more practical and responsible to get an artificial tree from now on.* Two days later I was standing in the middle of a big-box Christmas tree store, "Jingle Bells" blaring on the speakers, listening to my husband extol the virtues of fake-Frasers versus fake-Norfolks and did I want a six foot or eight foot plastic tree?—when I finally lost it. I broke down sobbing in the middle of a tropical paradise wilderness of physical and spiritual disorientation, and had to be led to the car. *I have got to get a grip,* I thought, despairing, *what is the matter with me?* It was time to figure out a way to embrace my new world.

Even in a society as highly mobile as our own has become, change is unsettling, discomfiting. Like our ancestors in faith, we are more often than not on the journey, in the wilderness, seeking to know who we are as a people, and trying to comprehend the God who, we hope, is going up with us—wherever it is we end up going.[2] The paths are not as familiar as they once were, and recognizable signposts are rare. It is easy to feel lost. The congregation I have now served for nearly twenty years has stayed fairly constant in size, but faces, accents, and styles change like a teenager choosing an outfit for a party. People do not stay put anymore, and the folk who find their way to church these days are hungry for a home, longing for community, and hoping the God of their long-vanished Sunday school childhoods can find the way to their latest change-of-address. *You are lucky,* observed one pastor friend after accepting a new call and uprooting his family for the third time in ten years, *you get to stay in the same place, and get a new congregation every five years anyway.*

Though it felt something less than lucky fifteen years ago, my Christmas-store epiphany was a most providential happening. Plopped down like a snowbird in the midst of the teeming, loud, intense, and tropical world of brazen Miami, I was instantly adrift. Old friends and family were a world away. The theology and pastoral training that had seemed so robust when I had planted them in the soil of my first congregation seemed alien, inappropriate. They struggled for life, then withered in strange soil. I

---

2. Exodus 33:15, NRSV. Moses speaking to God: *If your presence will not go, do not carry us up from here.*

was trying to grow daffodils in the tropics, and it was not working. The reliable continuity of the cycle of seasons had vanished without a trace, leaving me marooned in a world of eternal green, surrounded by flowers, fruits, and exotic scents that made for a fabulous vacation but a strange homecoming.

Slowly, I found myself turning to the seasons of the liturgical calendar for a sense of rhythm and order. The congregation I now served used a lectionary-based church school curriculum, and so, for the first time, I began to preach the three-year cycles of the Common Lectionary. Holy days I had never noticed before began to pop up in my spirit like orchids blooming after a long dry season. My first *Tres Reyes*, the annual Three Kings' Day celebration of the Hispanic communities of Miami, made Epiphany come alive for me; it was a festival I had previously noted only because the denominational calendar appointed it as an appropriate day for baptisms. Following the Star that year to the place where it came to rest, I was surprised to find myself coming home. There was incarnation in the pages of the *Miami Herald*; the life of the Christ was becoming flesh in the lives of my new congregation, in my fascinating adopted city, and even in me. Enthusiastically, I turned to the six-week fast of Lent, welcomed Easter, rediscovered Pentecost; and by the long summer's end, I found myself a new creation: no longer anticipating autumn and winter, but longing for Advent, eager to begin to trace the Story one more time.

Unfettered by the falling of leaves and the passing of common seasons, I now mark my time week by week, text by text, story by story, treading the well-worn path of the Christian year: Lent 2. The Sunday of the Transfiguration. Christmastide, Ordinary 17, the Reign of Christ. Festival Sundays provide well-lighted signs to mark the way: but in truth, it is the time between that I have come to treasure as manna from heaven, the Word-Made-Flesh: Ordinary Time, the habitat of the commonplace.

Now and again, miracle touches the lives and stories and words from God that these articles and sermons have attempted to honor and to recount—a dream almost forgotten, an inexplicable event, a whisper of the Divine breath—but more often than not, the "stuff" of the sermons I have preached week after week in this small congregation in Miami comes from the flotsam and jetsam of random, unremarkable, ordinary-time living. A story in the newspaper, an image from the evening news. A poem, a word, a fragment of thought. An event in my life, or in the lives of family or friends. A quiet tragedy endured by one or two but made bearable by the embracing arms of the people of God. A natural disaster endured, a conversation shared or overheard, a chance encounter with a stranger. A collision with a biblical text I thought I understood—but that was born again through an unexpected encounter with life and the living God who gives it.

In the end, these small things may not add up to much—but on the way through this wilderness, they are *manna* for me: the stuff of life, flakes scattered thickly across the desert floor. Day by day, they are gathered up by hopeful hands and placed gently into baskets of kindness and faithfulness until by grace, it is no longer *man hu?*—what is it?—but *manna*, the bread that God has given us to sustain us on our long road home.[3]

---

3. Exodus 16:15, NRSV.

2

The Scent of Incarnation

Advent and Christmastide

SOMETIMES I STILL LOOK for it, in the darkness of early winter evenings. The experience is so powerful that I cannot believe I cannot see it, touch it. But apart from an occasional, faint glimmering of white behind the limbs of a tree, I am not sure, exactly, *what* it looks like. I do not understand why it is there sometimes, but not others; and I am not sure I could even describe what it is like to someone who has never sensed it. I know I could never have imagined it, before I moved to South Florida and experienced it for myself. No manufactured perfume, however costly, could reproduce its affect. But the scent is unmistakable, exotic, intoxicating, enriching. I guess I have come to believe that it is a gift for Advent, or Christmas. Night blooming jasmine, like the odor of incarnation, comes unexpected on the night breezes for those who would open their senses and lift up their heads.

Each year, about this time, we all go looking, do we not?—senses open and straining for the faintest whiff of the difference that God's coming incarnation in Jesus of Nazareth might make in our world. *Emmanuel*, God with us, what does it mean? The Word made flesh . . . can we see it there, glimmering faintly in the darkness? What does this incarnation look like? How can we describe what we have felt, what we believe, to those who have never sensed it, or whose senses have become dulled by too much garish familiarity, the cheap cologne of commercial Christmas? Above all, if we were to risk going out into the darkness again, searching, can we be certain we will be able to find what we seek?

For those of us who year after year preach—or listen in on—the familiar texts of Advent and Christmas, a fresh uncovering of Advent expectation, Christmas newness, is a daunting, even deflating task. The themes—Judgment, Annunciation, Visitation, Incarnation—are as overplayed as "Jingle Bells." Besides, the Christmas season has been co-opted by popular culture to such a great degree that it often seems as if from Halloween onward Christmas is in hot pursuit of us—the Hound of Hollywood running us to ground, baying all the while—by sheer volume robbing us of the possibility of uncovering any fresh, delicate notes underneath the relentless onslaught of White Christmas and *peace-on-earth-good-will-to-men*.

We have been this way before, so many times that the last thing we want to do when we push back from the Thanksgiving table is go out looking for Christmas. Even in the Bible, the stories of Advent and Christmas—drawn from the well-plowed fields of Luke's first and second chapters and salted with the Gospel of John—present us with such a familiar cast of characters, such a frequently sung refrain, that finding a glimmer of the unexpected, *again*, would seem to be a veritable impossibility. It is perilously easy to permit these stories—the tales of Christmas—to be reduced to stock characters, a pat story line, foregone conclusions. The Childless Couple. The Angel Visitant. The Faithful Virgin. The Journey to Bethlehem. After all, we have been listening to these same stories for the whole of our lives, most of us, and we know them too well—certainly, well enough to hum along. Why should we pay attention? Why now? Would it really make a difference if this year, we sang it from memory, did it by rote?

Several years ago, while on a trip to New York City to visit my performer daughter, I had an opportunity to see The *Lion King* on Broadway. The last two times I had gone to New York, we were unable to secure tickets to any performance—the show was booked for months in advance. By some miracle, my daughter was able to acquire two coveted orchestra seats for an evening performance, and I planned the entire trip around the climax of seeing that show. Finally, it was happening.

The costuming was fantastic. The singing, fabulous. The staging, intricately beautiful. The interplay of puppetry, costume, actor, sound, and light, beguiling. I was entranced, captivated. I wept through the opening number, *Circle of Life*, as much for the fulfillment of my anticipation as for the theatrical magic unfolding around me. But as the show moved on, something happened. Everything was as I had imagined it to be—but it did not feel, well, *magical*. Irritated, I resisted my shift into boredom. I had paid a lot of money to see this show. I had waited years to be here. I was, by golly, gonna enjoy the main event, the culmination of my longing. I hunkered down, determined to be transported with delight. I failed. Do not get me wrong—I *liked* the show . . . but truth to tell, the magic I had longed for just was not there. Going out into the cold city night, my daughter, who had seen *Lion King* several times before, turned to me and said, *well?* And I said, as I was expected to say, as I had wanted to say, *it was wonderful, I loved it*. And she said flatly, *yeah, it's great*. And we fell silent while an icy wind off the river blew across us, odorless, passionless, chilling our spirits.

Then she lifted up her head and said, *do you know what bothers me? Did you notice that scene near the end, when everyone pours on stage from the aisles and the wings and they sing "He Lives in You," and Simba gains the courage to claim his heritage as king? That's supposed to be the climax of the second act, the heart of the story. And the first few times I saw it, it was breathtaking—the dancing, I just can't begin to describe how astonishing it was. What bothered me tonight was, well, they're doing it by rote. They've been singing and dancing it so long, they just don't care any more; they're going through the motions. And that is so sad. If it were me, I would be so grateful just to be a part of it, every moment I would dance and sing with all my heart.*

And I got it. When we stop paying attention, when the story becomes so familiar that we just go through the motions, the magic dies. The Spirit of Advent, the Life of Christmas cannot visit us . . . and it is no one's fault but our own. But—if we sing and dance with all our hearts? Immerse ourselves gladly and attentively in the repetition, the intricate details, the seemingly unrelated stories of minor characters? Sing as if the tale could not be told if our voice fell silent? Dance as if everyone were watching only us—as if the entire meaning of the story hinged on whether the audience believes that we believe in what we are doing and saying?

On the fourth Sunday of Advent, the choir at the church I pastor sang its annual Christmas cantata, while down on the floor of the sanctuary, church members dressed up in pageant clothes—bathrobes and muslin and tinsel—to enact the story of Christmas. Everyone rehearsed for weeks, until all the movements were familiar and comfortable, well-worn for singers and actors alike. They all wanted to get it right, to be ready, and they were. But at the same time, like John the Baptizer rehearsing his call for the coming one in the wilderness in the Gospel of John (1:14–34), the cast was utterly unprepared for the moment when it came. All of the faces were familiar: members known to one and all, down to the newborn girl playing baby Jesus—but when the woman playing Mary and the man playing Joseph discovered, that Sunday morning at 11:45, that there was still no room for them at the inn, the woman began to weep. Not acting, but genuine tears of helplessness and loss and grief. Watching from the balcony as they sang, the choir, too, began quietly to weep. The story was *real*; we were in the presence of holy mystery. When it was all over, and everybody was clearing the church to go home, an old woman in the congregation made her slow way up the steps to the chancel, looked down at the face in the manger—and leaned over and kissed the child. As the Gospel of John says, we ourselves did not know him, *but the Word became flesh, and dwelt among us, full of grace and truth. And we have beheld his glory.*[1]

ET INCARNATUS EST

We of the airless world await
caught throat and limb frozen
the unbegotten breath
breathless we watch:
the wind shimmered spirit invading
sinks incarnate and stricken
the air of us becoming
awakened, we gasp
first breath we draw
stunned, and start
at the scent of myrrh.

ADVENT

Luke 21:5-28 *Isaiah 65:17-25*

O Holy Nightmare

I used to have a recurring dream. It came the first time when I was maybe seventeen or eighteen years old, and thereafter, two or three times a year until I was around thirty. This was no vision of a new Jerusalem, like Isaiah's, but rather, more like that waking dream of Jesus, as he sat with his disciples dozing in the afternoon sun outside the Temple and saw a vision

---

1. John 1:14, NRSV.

The Scent of Incarnation

of calamity, a holy nightmare. In this dream, I am around eleven years old, living with my family on an Air Force base in Oklahoma. Outside playing in a field near my home, I am enjoying the sun and fresh air when, without warning, a siren begins to howl. It is the civil defense siren, and its terrible wailing fills the air around me. Is it a tornado? I look around for a funnel cloud, but the sky is clear. Are there missiles on the horizon? Is this how a nuclear war begins? I begin running for home, suddenly conscious that the field and my whole neighborhood are deserted. I am afraid. When I reach the safety of my front door, I burst through it, yelling for my mother, my father, my brother. No one answers, and my voice sounds small next to the deafening scream of the siren. In the living room, the television set is on, displaying the yellow civil defense triangle. I drag a mattress from my brother's bed, crawl into the bathtub, and wait. The siren goes on and on, and I am alone. Each time I awaken from this dream, I am terrified.

In a sunny courtyard in Jerusalem, long ago, the disciples were idly observing how beautiful, how comfortingly permanent God's Temple seemed, when Jesus, spurred by some vision only he could see, plunged them without warning into the realm of holy nightmare.

The days will come, he said, *when not one stone will be left upon another.* And a chill came over the afternoon. The Temple, still glowing golden in the sunlight, seemed suddenly vulnerable, fragile, unreal. Their voices cracking with mingled fear and disbelief, the shaken disciples turned to Jesus: *when? And by what sign shall we know that the time is near?*[2]

But Jesus will not—maybe cannot—tell them. He cannot comfort them with signs and timetables, seven year balanced budget projections, schedules for the end of the world. Instead, he draws them into a terrible vision, culled from the worst nightmares of the Jewish people's memories of disasters past, their darkest prophetic hours, and embellished by new and terrible images, specific to the disciples' emerging identity as people of the way. It is as if the worst fears of the entire community were gathered into one terrible, apocalyptic, unholy nightmare.

For Jesus does not simply see a community approaching a crossroads of judgment: a time of reckoning brought about by his impending trial and crucifixion. No, this vision of Jesus is far-sighted, long-range, and immensely serious. Jesus looks at the temple, and at his fragile community of disciples, and foresees a time when virtually all the structures of com-

---

2. Luke 21:6–7, NRSV.

munity and religion and creation will crumble and fall: leaving the people of God wholly dependent upon faith's slender lifeline—a lifeline they have exercised far too infrequently, and not well.

The people of Luke's time heard these words and saw them brought to terrible life during the Roman siege of Jerusalem and Palestine, a time near the end of the first century when, the historian Josephus recorded, over a million inhabitants of golden Jerusalem perished, and the survivors were driven to cannibalism in order to survive.

And we hear them, some two thousand years later, and see a line drawn in the sand, the whole world pausing on an indrawn breath ... and we are not only sitting in church on a sunny morning in late November, we are huddled in a small house on the outskirts of Baghdad, wondering whether today will be the end of the world. We do not have to look about us for signs: we are twenty cruise missiles and a rogue nuke away from becoming the inheritors of nightmare, and we can do little about it.

Does it seem that the solid walls of our private temple seem secure? They are not for everyone ... and we know it, as week after week we lift our small voices in prayer for the ruined hopes of people whose lives are torn by natural disaster; the wounded possibilities for peace in Israel and Palestine; a failing marriage; the life of a friend with cancer; a small boy dying of a brain tumor fifteen hundred miles away from his home; a way out of military necessity in Iraq. In our secret hearts, we know that our lives, and the lives of those we love, are shielded from the storm by the thinnest of membranes, or perhaps not at all.

Maybe that warning of distant thunder is what Jesus heard, that long-ago day. Heard it, and looked at his disciples with love, wanting to warn them: *the world isn't a safe place, but you will be safe*. There is a forecast of clouds on the horizon—but with it, a flash of grace, like lightening, in the gathering storm.

And that flash of grace is the heart of the reality toward which Jesus points, even in the face of uncertainty and loss. *Do not be terrified*, he affirms. *Not a hair on your head will perish.*[3] *Stand up and raise your heads, for your redemption is drawing near.*

Honestly, this is not my first instinct. When I was a child growing up on air force bases in the 1950s and '60s, another response altogether was drilled into me: *duck and cover*. But the sad fact is, *duck and cover* is hardly

---

3. Luke 21:9, 18, NRSV.

something any of us need to be taught. For we are born with a need to see to our own safety . . . and most of our sad and civilized culture lives by that rule, and that rule alone. The way we vote, the way we use our money, what we say to the people around us, how we keep silence when we should speak . . . it is all *duck and cover*, one way or another.

But the gospel of Jesus—that is to say, the *good news*—is that we are not bound by our culture when we are bound to God. We have the freedom to admit that hiding under a desk will not save us—nor a bigger closet, a larger gun, a healthier portfolio or a move out of the city, into the country. That we even believed for a minute that such things could save us is laughable, really, absurd. What a relief to relinquish that fantasy, and to acknowledge at last that we will not be saved until, in the midst of it all, we can *look up and raise our heads*.[4]

With the certainty of a child who knows how to find his way home, Jesus finds that place in the heart of God—where no physical reality, however threatening, can harm. He turns to his followers, and, loving them, affirms: you are the New Jerusalem, the Temple, the place of safety where the work of God will be made sure. Be brave.

Attending a recent regional church meeting, I listened while a member of the congregation I serve was examined as a candidate for ministry. During her testing by the presbytery, the candidate remarked that when she left home to study at Princeton, one of the ministers had said to her, *I hope seminary won't ruin you.* And she puzzled for a year over what he meant by that comment, and what it would mean to be ruined by preparing for the gospel ministry. And then she said to us, *Now I know that I have been ruined by seminary, and it is a good thing. Because God uses ruined things. God's work is done in ruination. A broken body on a cross, broken bread. Ruined lives, available for God to make a new thing. I am glad God has ruined me.* Listening to her, I knew she was bearing witness to something important and vital and true about our lives as people of God: something we would perhaps rather not acknowledge altogether openly, but something that can save us. Just this: that the way of Jesus winds through places of ruination and hopelessness to claim and to call us into the honest reign of God in this world, a place of the heart where there is peace and wholeness and possibility—not despite the ruining of our lives but because of it.

---

4. Luke 21:28, NRSV.

Isaiah's folk—there at the end of an era, with their fingernails broken and their hands bruised and their backs aching with the hard and thankless labor of rebuilding a ruined city while the rubble still stood thigh-high in the streets—they knew that place, and they sang: *I am about to create Jerusalem as a joy and its people as a delight! I will rejoice in Jerusalem and delight in my people. Oh, be glad and rejoice forever in what I am creating, for I am about to create a new heavens and a new earth!*[5] It is the people of God, ruined at last, and knowing it.

It was not until a few years ago that I finally noticed: sometime, somehow, I had stopped dreaming that terrible nightmare of lonely holocaust. Sometime, when I was busy with other things, God got busy too, and drove away the fear of the little child that was in me. Maybe, finally, I began to let myself be ruined for God. I don't know precisely how or when or even why it happened. But the terror of the night passed away, and not only my head, but also my heart was lifted up, so that in the midst of ruination or outside it, I believe the words of Jesus and the song of Isaiah: *not a hair on your heads will perish, for they shall not hurt nor destroy in all my holy mountain, says the Lord.*

ADVENT

Mark 13:24–37   *Matthew 1:12–25*

The Invisible Man

With the lighting of one candle, we begin the church year and remind ourselves that we are not on the world's time. It must have been a theological cynic who thought up Advent as the liturgical first season: where week-by-week as the season deepens, we light another candle while it grows darker and darker.

Did I say *cynic*? Maybe I should have said genius, or at the very least, *acute observer of the signs of the times*. For things have not much changed in the world since the author of the Gospel of Mark recorded how Jesus' disciples sat him down in the courtyard of the Jerusalem Temple a few days before his arrest and death and asked him, *what are the signs for when all this shall be accomplished?* The news was bad, and getting worse. Jesus, anticipating his own impending death, described for his closest

---

5. Isaiah 65:17–19, NRSV.

friends a world in which even the established flow of times and seasons would be catastrophically shaken: the stars falling like pearls from a broken necklace, the sun and moon dimmed in their courses, the suffering of the cosmos echoing the suffering of a beleaguered people of God as the cry of the dying Jesus echoed off the stone walls of Jerusalem—*my God, my God, why have you forsaken me?* Mark's own day, some thirty years later, was even worse: the infant church and its Jewish mother scattering for survival into the caves and wildernesses of Judah as the mad emperor of Rome turned his malevolent eye on those stubborn monotheists who would not bow the knee to Caesar.

And the signs of our times?

The sad eyes of African children, orphaned by the pandemic of AIDS, passively awaiting their own deaths. The still-desolate neighborhoods of New Orleans, two years after Hurricane Katrina. Test results that tell us that once again, the cancer has recurred. The war in Iraq, the deepening darkness of genocide in Darfur. Too many threats, no real solutions. A boat, paint peeling and sails frayed, disgorging hungry and desperate Haitian refugees into the rough surf to struggle ashore into the waiting arms of strangers who know their small acts of kindness may be the only welcome these would-be immigrants receive, before they are gathered up, processed, and deported. These are the signs of the times, signs at which sensible people head for the storm cellar, bolt the doors tight, and hunker down in the darkness with their hands over their ears, trying to shut out the howling of the wind and the pounding of hailstones on the tin roof.

Lighting candles, we begin the year in darkness, waiting out in the open for signs that, once they have come, do not bring us hope but rather, haunt our dreams. Ask for a sign? *Ask?*

I don't think so.

On this Advent Sunday morning, with the signs of the times beating like a storm against the windows of our sanctuary, with one small candle flickering bravely against the darkness, we turn to the story of Joseph, the invisible man: the only soul in the Christmas story for whom unexpected signs came not as a welcomed gift of good news on the horizon, but rather, as a portent of disaster and the crushing of life's hope.

Have you ever noticed where Joseph stands in most manger scenes? Behind Mary, a ways back from the baby upon whom every eye is fixed except his. He is outside the circle of light, waiting in the dark, his gaze turned inward. Not quite adoring, not a bit sure of his role in this gauzy tale of God and angels and miracles; barely accepting the "sign" that has shattered the life he once thought would be his. In my nativity set, Joseph stands alone, his arms folded across his chest—evidence, I guess, that Joseph, like us, does not go gently into that good night.

Joseph is the invisible man—a man, I think, a lot like you and me. An honorable soul, trying to get along in life, obeying the rules and hoping others would do the same. Hoping in his humble way that the world, like his own heart and hearth, would be a good place, an honorable place, a place of order and fairness and peace. But a young woman was with child; and the world, his world, became suddenly untidy, hostile, unfair. What to do?

Joseph, seeking order in a world gone suddenly insane, appealed (as most of us will) to the rule of law. Hoping, as we do, that by so doing he could find again a world that made sense and his place in that world. He did not ask for a sign. He merely considered[6]—what is the right thing to do? The legal thing? To stay? To go? To punish? To forgive? Signs, after all, are so hard to come by, and messy, when you think about it. So Joseph consulted his attorney and his conscience and determined an appropriate course of action. Legal, but not devoid of compassion. Right, but not self-righteous. He did not ask for a sign, but he thought it all through, and he had the rule of law to back him up.

And this is what Joseph would have done with the birthing of Emmanuel, the God who had in this way hoped to be with us: *He resolved to dismiss her quietly, and spare her public disgrace.* And that might have been the end of it—surely for Joseph, but perhaps for Mary and her unborn son as well: just another impoverished, disgraced, single mother, trying to fend for herself in a harsh and unforgiving world. But then—there was a sign. Or, to be more precise, there was a dream. *And the angel of the Lord appeared to Joseph and said, "Joseph, son of David, do not be afraid to take Mary for your wife, for the child conceived in her is from the Holy Spirit."*[7] Joseph dreamed, and when he was done, he woke up to a world that was changed. He had not asked for a sign, but a sign had been given anyway, because when God wants to be with us, *Emmanuel,* God is like that. And Joseph, the invisible man, that sensible and proper soul, turned out to be more of a dreamer than he thought . . . and he let it be. He laid aside the proper thing, the tidy thing, the legal thing, and, letting disorder stand, he

---

6. Matthew 1:19, NRSV.
7. Matthew 1:20, NRSV.

made Mary a home. And in the midst of that brave act of disorder; in that quiet act of defiance against the rule of law; in that hopeful investment in the new world of dreams and signs, suddenly, there was *Emmanuel*: God with Joseph, God with Mary, God in Jesus the Christ, God with us.

At Texas A & M where my brother went to school, my dad tells me there is an old legend, dating back to the early years of the great football rivalries of Texas universities. It happened that when the members of the team were counted up on the field just before the kickoff, the Aggies were found to be one man short. What to do? Without that man, the team was incomplete, and the game, forfeit. The stadium sat breathless, waiting, despairing.

Suddenly, a boy ran out of the stands and onto the sidelines, where he suited up and took the empty place on the field. The game commenced, and, of course, the Aggies won. But the boy who saved the day is not remembered: he is the invisible man. Rather, Aggies will tell you when this story is told: *You are the twelfth man.* That is, everyone who watches, everyone who hears, everyone and anyone who shows up: *you are the twelfth man,* and without you, the game cannot be won.

The first Advent season that I was in ministry, I served as the associate pastor of an old, affluent, once prestigious congregation in upstate New York. The pastor of the church, a man of deeply felt convictions, had crafted with his own hands a massive Advent wreath made entirely of strands of twisted and tangled barbed wire. The reason for the symbol, I learned, was this: In the early '80s, the signs of the times were bad, and the pastor was a disillusioned soul, frustrated with his congregation's lack of passion for justice, and with his own seeming inability to awaken them to the works of the kingdom. In bitterness he wove his wreath, and jammed the purple candles so deeply into the dark mass of twisted wire that it seemed to me they were almost invisible from the pews, their light hidden in a hard, tangled darkness. The congregation was enraged, for no one in that old cathedral church thought that a barbed wire wreath was an appropriate way to mark the Christmas season—and secretly, I agreed.

But now, I have come to believe that *that* marking—indeed, that Mark's old Gospel itself—is an important part of the mystery of darkness and light that we name the season of Advent. For we are invisible women and men, lighting candles in a world that week by week seems to grow darker, lighting candles and waiting with resignation—no, rather, with hope—for the morning to come.

And rather than waiting in denial that the darkness is real, we step out of the shadows into the small circle of light, taking our place with Joseph, taking our place as the Twelfth Man so that the game can go on and the kingdom come.

Maybe a barbed wire wreath is not such a bad symbol after all: if we could just focus less on the mess that holds our candles secure, and more on the light shining in the darkness. For on Christmas Eve that cold, dark season, I could see, even from the back of the sanctuary, how the light caught on the sharp points and edges of the tangled wire—the warm glow of the candles' flame shattering into a hundred sparkling points of light, so that there was enough light for all. Enough to shine on the face of Joseph, enough to shine on us—enough, even, to shine through us, on the world. *And what I say to you, I say to all: Watch!*[8]

ADVENT

Isaiah 11:1–10 *Matthew 3:1–12*

Baptizing the Bulgarians

It is easy to enter this gospel story this morning with a certain sense of smugness—and what a relief, after our perilous journey, these past couple of weeks, through texts of judgment, apocalypse, and damnation! Easy, because Matthew makes it so clear that we, his readers, are *nothing* like the odd lot of characters inhabiting this story of preparation for the coming of Jesus of Nazareth the Christ: nothing like that oddball John the Baptist, wilderness prophet and purveyor of the bizarre; nothing like the Pharisees and Sadducees who trekked down from golden Jerusalem to make their show of public piety before the prophet and the people who followed him.

How much more removed from this story could we be, as we sit here on a mild and sunny South Florida morning, happy in our beautifully decorated sanctuary and bathed in a gentle sense of Christmas anticipation? We have baptized two beloved children of our church this day, but even that theological connection cannot bring us closer to this primitive Jordan River revival scene of baptism and repentance where John the Baptizer's very demeanor screams *I'm not one of you! I'm different!*

---

8. Mark 13:37, NRSV.

The Scent of Incarnation

Girded with camel's hair, belted with leather, consuming a healthy, natural diet of locusts and wild honey—surely high in protein, if a tad crunchy—raving about repentance and judgment, John the Baptist is the very antithesis of custom and authority, a primitive throwback to a more dangerous and primal time. Not for him the reasoned and careful lives of the Pharisees, bounded by rules and regulations. Not for him, the polished, perfumed and elegant lives of the Sadducees, secure in their Jerusalem palaces. No, John's allegiance was to an older, starker world, when the prophets of God strode the desert pathways and the lives of the people of the land were edged with an untamed, sacred glory.

The cost of civilization had worn down the people of God. The practice of piety had exhausted them. And is it any wonder that John's stark message, vibrating as it was with the vitality of truth, sent them by droves out from the safety of the city's walls, down through the dry and rocky countryside until several days' journey brought them at last to the waters of the Jordan, lifeblood of Israel, and to the prophet John? They wanted something new, something real. The life they had wasn't cutting it; the piety they professed was a tired remnant of something they could only scarcely remember, a pallid remnant of a faith their souls still yearned for with an intensity that was sometimes frightening. They wanted to feel alive. They *needed* to know God. And so—*they were baptized by him in the river Jordan*, Matthew tells us, *confessing their sins*. And strangely, the Pharisees and the Sadducees, keepers of the Tradition, came too. Why?

Matthew wants us to believe that the Pharisees and the Sadducees had no good reason for making that journey to the Jordan, seeking John. Using the scathing denunciation of John—*you brood of vipers, who warned you to flee from the wrath to come?*—Matthew sets us up to dismiss the seeking of the Pharisees and Sadducees as politically motivated, hypocritical, insincere.[9] We are not like them—no, we, like the people of the land who followed the message of the Baptist, are sincere seekers, turning our backs on a religion of empty tradition, repenting of our past alliances and becoming, by grace, the hope of the future of the faith. We are not like *them*.

Are we?

The Gospel of Matthew, it seems, would like us to believe that the appearance of the Pharisees and the Sadducees at John's riverside revival was empty, vain posturing, devoid of any potential for genuine transfor-

---

9. Matthew 3:7, NRSV.

mation. He would probably have liked the bumper sticker pointed out to me by a friend, and seen by me at a no less ironic place than the golf course at the Coral Gables Country Club last week. *Jesus is Coming Soon,* it read, *Look Busy.* If Matthew were here today, he would probably have enjoyed plastering that slick message across the Mercedes', BMWs, and Range Rovers of the Pharisees and the Sadducees. They did not want to repent, they only wanted to *look* busy, in order to impress the people. And if we believe him, we will be safe when we read this text, for we will be able to dismiss out of hand the unsettling similarities between our own lives and those of these demonized, derided characters.

My rabbi friend reminded me this week that I saw in the Old City of Jerusalem last summer the ruins of the homes of the Sadducees snuggled up against the buried walls of the Temple of Herod. They were the homes of the upper middle class, religiously responsible city dwellers. They were our homes, the homes of sincere people who were blessed with a certain measure of affluence, influence, and means. They were *not* the homes of people who needed to abandon the city for a dangerous three-day walk into the Galilee—or down to the Red Sea, depending on whose commentary you read—just to make a public show of piety.

Indeed, if you look at Matthew's text with a certain degree of healthy suspicion, you will, I believe, begin to suspect as I do, that Matthew's denunciation of the Pharisees and the Sadducees had more to do with ideology than with accuracy. Ask yourself, *what kind of prestige is there to be gained in a muddy river among a haphazard gathering of ordinary citizens at a riverside revival?* Prestige, if they needed more of it, was in Jerusalem, not in the wilderness. Recognition was to be found where the people who mattered were—not out in the middle of nowhere, sitting in the mud with nobodies.

No, I think we have to acknowledge that those John denounced as a "brood of vipers" were as sincere as anyone else seeking baptism by John in the Jordan in that season of new possibility; and, having admitted that, I have to allow further that this story is not as far from us as we would like to believe.

Because if they were sincere seekers, as serious in their baptism as we are in our own, then what happened? And more troubling, if it happened to them, isn't it possible it could happen to us as well?

I search the footnotes, ponder the commentaries and the Bible stories, and still can't stop wondering about them: *what went wrong?* Was

John just a little too bizarre, his appearance not quite respectable enough to cause them to take his message seriously, in the end? Was the press and the weight and the comfortable habit of the way things were too ingrained to allow for the possibility of starting over? Were responsibilities back home in Jerusalem too overwhelming, too time-consuming, too distracting from the task of giving their new spirituality the time and effort it needed to take root and grow? Did they remember their baptism in the Jordan with nostalgia and a twinge of regret, like we recall a vanished moment when we had vowed that *this* time, our lives would be different, that we would make our time on this planet really count for something, and for someone?

Too many things can happen in our lives to derail us from our sincere desire to have lives grounded in a rich spirituality. A smug belief that we are different, that it will not happen to us. So many challenges, so many distractions. Old beliefs, older habits. A yearning spirit smothered by exhaustion, preoccupation, and a lack of self-discipline. So much time and water under the bridge from the time that we arose, joyful and dripping with grace, from the waters of our baptism, determined to live always as a people of the way of Jesus. Just one more missed chance, another footnote in the dusty pages of some forgotten church register.

In Israel, near one of the two places that tradition says John baptized in the Jordan River, there is a tourist way station, and a small set of steps by which pilgrims can descend into the waters of the river, seeking to find where Jesus was baptized, and experience a connection, a place for faith to come alive. Near that spot, not quite accurately but covering the necessary contingencies, the Israelis have placed a small bronze plaque: *On or somewhere near this site, Jesus of Nazareth baptized.*

When our group from a Miami synagogue stopped there this summer, the rabbi announced over the bus's speaker: *the Reverend Laurie Kraus is one of our group members, and she is a Christian minister who will be glad to explain baptism to you.* And I was. I explained how baptism is done in the church of Jesus Christ, and why. I described the methods of baptism, and the ways in which it was connected to the ancient traditions of the Jewish people, and more contemporarily, to the *mikvah*, the ritual bath one woman from our group had taken just the morning before, preparing for her conversion. I did, I think, a careful and a thorough job. When we went through the souvenir store to the river, we were passed by a group of tourists, speaking in a language I could not identify, dressed in white smocks with tacky pictures of Jesus silk-screened across the belly. Now, throughout our time in Palestine and Israel, I had been fascinated by the diversity of cultures and languages represented by citizens and tourists. I tried to identify each group, and, when I could not, asked my husband, *where do you think they're from? What language is that?* Soon growing tired of my linguistic badgering, he came to reply to every query, *they're from Bulgaria*. An older lady who had attached herself to my family listened in, nodding knowingly each time my husband spoke. Back at the Galilean tourist station, our group stood on the overlook at the River Jordan, still avidly discussing Christian baptism, and watched the tourists settle themselves on the steps in the river in their pilgrim smocks, laughing and splashing water over themselves while their friends took pictures. My companions from the synagogue in Miami, looking concerned, pressed nearer to me. *We thought you said there had to be a minister or a priest*, they said. *What are they doing down there in the water? You didn't tell us about this kind of baptism.* Piously, I announced that, whatever those people were doing, it was not baptism, and I turned away—more than a little disgruntled that the splashing tourists had ruined my scholarly Christian object lesson.

But as I turned, a hand touched my arm, and a small voice began to speak softly. *Well, maybe since they don't have priests, maybe because they're in a communist country, maybe they have to baptize themselves.*

What? I turned to the elderly lady, my family's adoptee, who was speaking. Noticing my frown, she elaborated timidly, *well, they're the Bulgarians, right?*

Who knows? Maybe that old Jewish lady knew more about baptism than I do. Maybe the "Bulgarians"—or whoever they were—had it right. Maybe to splash in joy and to take responsibility for baptizing yourself is a way of Jesus that we ought to attend, a way that could keep the story of the church from vanishing unnoticed from the pages of faith, just another forgotten footnote in the annals of global spirituality. To immerse ourselves, while our friends and neighbors cheer us on, in a more enveloping sense of participation in what we do and what we believe. To go wherever we must, descending whatever stair, in order to find what we seek, and possess it, and to do it with playfulness and joy. To permit no system, no denomination, no pastor, no church, to do for us what God has called us to do for ourselves and for God's kin-dom: to repent, to turn again, and to proclaim the coming of the Lord.[10]

Jesus is coming soon—get busy. Amen.

ADVENT

Zephaniah 3:14–20   Luke 3:7–18

The Six-Toed Jesus

*So, with many other exhortations,
he proclaimed good news to the people.
Luke 3:18*

She was, in short, the most disagreeable old woman I had ever met. *That's Miss Murch*, she snapped like a proclamation, whenever she was introduced. *By choice, not by necessity*, she would always add, though, knowing her, it was difficult to credit *that* assertion. Miss Arlene Murch hated everyone; the pastor with whom I worked told me that I should not take it personally. And it did seem true. In visit after visit, she recounted her litany of complaints against the world: Her neighbors were loud and rude, trying to keep her awake at night. Her landlord was trying to throw her out on the street, though she was, of course, a model tenant. Her pastor was a clod, who never attended to her needs. The choir director had not asked her to sing in the choir and all her friends were backbiting old biddies, whom she did not trust, no, not one little bit. One Christmas Eve, trying to be nice, I walked up to wish her a merry Christmas. She looked fragile in the candlelight—a small woman, alone, surrounded by darkness. *Merry Christmas, Arlene*, I said. She tried to smile, her face cracking with the effort. Her eyes filled with tears, her hands tightened on my arms for a moment, then dropped to her sides. She tried to speak, cleared her throat, then shook her head and walked away.

Is it possible to come to Christmas as we are—as we *really* are? Not like the babe in Bethlehem, newborn and pure, free of mistakes, failures, the accumulated weariness of years of trying and trying again? Can we come to Christmas as that old woman did, with our imperfections cruelly

---

10. "kin-dom" is a term coined by mujerista theologian Ada Maria Isasi-Diaz as an inclusive rendering of the kingdom, or reign of God.

visible, defensive and desperate, offering only the flawed and fragile gift of ourselves?

If we could come to Christmas as newborn souls, clean and clear—how easy it would be to embrace the nativity of Christ as the season of expectation . . . to begin our living again, each Advent, as those who have thrown away last year's journal, stained and torn, and opened the leather cover of a new one, the pen of our lives poised over an unwritten, pristine page. But it is far too late to begin anew, even if we could . . . even if we would . . . for if we were really honest with ourselves, a God who could only take us with the slate clean is no god big enough for the world we live in or the loads we carry. But will a god who really knows us as we are really want us, or dare to dwell within us?

Enter John the Baptist, stalking down the line of those who had come to wait for him, narrowing his eyes speculatively. It is a hard beginning, a terrifying one. Hiding their imperfections, their fear, they had undertaken the long, dry journey to the desert to pay their respects, to prepare the way. They were respectable people, even successful. Their fears and follies were well hidden under a patina of genuine hope, their fragility deep in the closet. They looked right, and they were doing the right things. But somehow, John has outed them—seen them for what they truly are, and now what? We, who had already suspected that a God who knew us as we really are would have no use for us, we read these words and shrink, as they must have, to the back of the crowd . . . hoping to slip away again, evading Christmas judgment, before anyone notices we were there.

But the voice comes again, soft but relentless, not letting one of us get away . . . *you think you know who you are? You think you have your priorities straight? You belong to the family of God? God could raise out of rubble on the street, children better than you.*[11] No one is spared from his scathing diatribe, and strangely enough, no one tries. It is, after all, no less than we had thought of ourselves, and in a way, it is a relief to have it out in the open, to know where we stand. And that should have been the end of it: the pink slip at the office, the process server with a summons at the door, the "dear John" letter lying like a bomb in the mailbox. The End.

But this is a Christmas story, a gospel . . . and so, against all hope, the end is also the beginning, though not as we had imagined. First one, and then another steps out of the faceless crowd to admit what he is, to

---

11. Luke 3:7–8, paraphrased.

shrug off hopelessness, and to shoulder the responsibility of change. A tax collector steps forward, and then a soldier: *What should I do?* A mother of four, a painter. A teacher, a retiree, a school child, a lawyer: *and we, what should we do?*

And John said,

> *Bear fruits worthy of repentance. Turn, and live a different way. Give up the stuff that's cluttering up your life. If you have too many coats, give one to someone who has none. If your security has depended upon having power over others, give it up. If your growing bank account is all the security you have, quit stockpiling and try giving, for a change. Stop hiding yourself, and start this advent journey from where you are, not from where you wish you could be.*[12]

Are we listening? Can we hear that strident call for what it is?

We have understood *Repent*! to mean we must become something *else*, rather than more truly what we already are. But God is extending an open hand, not the pointed finger of accusation we fear. When God judges us, God judges us for good, inviting us to renounce those habits and hell-holes that hamper our soul's freedom—but we, misunderstanding, renounce ourselves, denounce others. God names what is broken within that we may turn and be healed, but we turn instead to self-hatred. God challenges us to find the courage to turn within, to give ourselves over to a self-examination that will free us like a cleansing fire, but we give up. But God has not given up on us. Judgment is not condemnation, and self-hatred is not the same as being born again. Listen to John, and look at those who have come—they are the ones who are willing to acknowledge who they are and what they need to be whole again.

They are bearing their hurt, their hunger, like a label: a *tax collector*—an enemy of the people, burdened by the knowledge that his actions are hurting his neighbors. A *soldier*—the servant of an oppressive regime who knows that power is no answer after all. *A crowd of people* who know in their hearts they have fallen short of the person they intended and hoped to become: a divorcee, who believes she is a failure at relationship. A father who doesn't see his kids enough. A businessman, downsized and wondering whether if he had just performed better, worked longer hours, whatever, they would have recognized his value. An old woman, close to tears on Christmas Eve, pushing love away with both hands. Look at them.

---

12. Luke 3:10–14, paraphrased.

And look at us, at who we are and how we hurt for the failures, great and small, of our lives, hearing not just the call of John but also the hopeful, helpful response of those who came—*and we, what should we do?*

This *is* good news. Good news, because John preached that God has not given up on us, as we have given up on ourselves. God does not believe that we are hopelessly lost in sin, and the world with us: God knows we are not worthless. God believes that we can turn, begin again, not as a little child but scarred and scared as we are, full of the presence of God as with light. God still believes it.

In Hebron, Texas, near where my parents live, there is a small old country church beside a busy road. Almost entirely overtaken by suburbia, and overshadowed by two shiny, new, aggressively contemporary churches that stand nearby, its shabby clapboard walls and fading paint could be easily overlooked and readily scorned. Within, however, there is a stained glass window, crafted in the early twentieth century by an immigrant glassmaker named Herbert Davis. Jesus stands with his arms outstretched, welcoming the needy that kneel and grasp at his robes. He is dressed, as is customary, all in white, but prominently figured in the lower center of the frame is a large, dirty foot with six toes. Herbert Davis, says a third-generation glassworker whose father worked with the artist, was born with a birth defect... and he liked to put six toes on Jesus because he had six toes, too. *Christ shares my humanity*, the picture says, *and I share his.*

Just before Christmas break, I drove my daughter over to the middle school so she could set up her harp for the holiday concert—her first performance as a member of the school orchestra. Featured that evening were two bands, a chorus, a jazz brass ensemble, the advanced orchestra, and the beginning orchestra—fourteen violins, three violas, two cellos, and one harp—all tuned to a different concert "A." From my place in the bleachers, I saw the orchestra conductor lean over and whisper something to my daughter, who shrugged, and then nodded. An hour and a half later, the announcement came: *we have a special treat this evening. For the first time, our middle school orchestra features a harpist. Before the final number, she will play a Christmas solo.* The room, filled with hundreds of young musicians and their families, fell silent. The girl set her hands to the strings and began to play: *silent night, holy night.* My eyes filled with tears as she moved through the song. *Holy infant so tender and mild.* At the phrase *sleep in heavenly peace*, her hand, slick with nerves, slipped on the strings and struck the wrong chord. Imperceptibly to anyone but me, her hands shook, as if to throw off the bad notes. She tried again—once, twice, and finally, eons later, finished the song. Straight-backed, she sat through the final all-orchestra finale, and then, the concert was over. I went down to the floor of the gym where she was packing up her instrument. Her eyes were full of unshed tears. Lifting her chin, she glared at me and said, *if you say I played well, I will never speak to you again*. Words of congratulation died on my lips, as I understood that my child required of me the gift of hard truth, the gift of John the Baptist. I swallowed hard. *Next time you'll do better*, I said, and the tears spilled over. I opened my arms, and she laid her head on my shoulder and cried. The sounds of excited voices and shouted Christmas greetings faded around us, and we were alone in a wilderness of painful truth, potent love, and the fragile possibility of beginning again. Together, we walked out into the purple darkness, put her instrument into the trunk of the car, and drove home. The gaudy pink lights of the mall winked and flared beside us, promising all manners of store-bought happiness—but around us, the night was dark and still, and the promise of Christmas was real.

CHRISTMAS EVE

Luke 1:26–38, 46–56   *After the Angels*

When all is said and done, the way God is born among us, at Christmas or any time, should be glorious. That is why it is such a wondrous gift to celebrate a baptism on this Sunday of Christmas Eve: an act of celebration and promise in the fullness of a season of glorious possibility. We carefully plan, together with the child's parents, this deep celebration of God's faithfulness and our obedience to Christ's command. We proclaim the promises of God, and make faithful promises in return; and in a moment, a little girl's life is set apart for the presence of God, holy. Surely this is also the point of the stories about Mary and Elizabeth in the Gospel of Luke. The scenes of preparation for the birth narratives of Jesus are detailed, careful, specific. It was in the days of Herod of Judea. Zechariah was a priest, descended from Abijah. Elizabeth, out of the house of Aaron. Joseph, from the house of David. It was in the sixth month, in a town of Galilee called Nazareth. With exquisite care the scene is presented, the groundwork laid. All is as it should be, the characters established with regard to position and lineage, history and heritage. The stage is set for a glorious beginning, and as the angel Gabriel descends, all fire and passion and shimmering power, there is a holy glory, in truth.

The tale he tells the girl is overwhelming, awesome, as well. *You shall conceive and bear a son. He shall be great. And he shall be called the Son of the Most High, and the Lord God will give to him the throne of his ancestor David. And he will reign over the house of Jacob forever, and of his kingdom there will be no end. The Holy Spirit will come upon you, and the power of the Most High will overshadow you, and the child will be called the Son of God.*[13] In the time of preparation, all is glorious: all is pregnant with power and magnificently holy. One can well believe that God had indeed visited and redeemed the people—one can well believe that even a girl might play a part in that great drama of salvation upon which the curtain is about to rise. Mary herself, caught up in the splendor of it all, agrees: yes! she says eagerly. *Yes, I am the servant of the Lord. Let it be to me according to your will.* The glory of it all is almost too much to bear, and we can scarcely wait for the next scene, except when we learn what it is. *Then*, Luke goes on, *the angel departed from her.*[14]

The angel departed from her, and the girl was left alone. And isn't that the way it always goes? You find the career of your dreams, and then the angel departs, and you have to get up and go to work every day of your life for the next fifty years. The child you longed for comes into your world, but the angel departs, and moments of parental glory are soon scattered carelessly over a field strewn with heartbreak and hard work, negotiation and sacrifice, fear and trembling. You fall in love, and then the angel departs and you have to learn to live with a stranger. The glory is an astonishment, a holy fire, an inspiration: but when the light fades and the curtain rises for the next act, the angel has departed, and always, the girl is alone.

Then a curious thing happens. Suddenly, all those matters that had seemed so carefully worked out, so solid and trustworthy, become . . . indefinite. Though all of the others in this story are rooted in history and lineage, the girl is not. She is merely Mary, a virgin. Though in preparation for the angel's momentous message details have been attended to with meticulous care—when the angel departs, so does the story's sense of clarity and precision. Now, the lonely girl goes "in those days" to "a Judean town." Where, we do not know. Just exactly when, we are not told. It is as

---

13. Luke 1:31–35, NRSV.
14. Luke 1:38, NRSV.

if some giant hand has obliterated the details, wiped the slate, turned off the lights, and left us in the dark. For the angel has departed, and now the working out of this momentous and holy matter rests on the narrow shoulders of a pregnant girl fleeing to a small village someplace in rural Judea. The power of the Most High had overshadowed her; but now the power that overshadows is an altogether darker thing of fear, uncertainty, and the possibility that things might not turn out for glory after all.

How can she bear it? How can we bear the risk of incarnation when the angel always goes away, and we are left alone to pick up the pieces and do the work and stumble through the fog and the frenzy, hoping against hope that we are on the right track, and that the favor of God, once so clear, has not now deserted us forever? What do we do when the shadow we see is not the shadow of the Most High, but something else altogether? We know that shadow, we see it every day. We see it in sickness, we see it in grief. We see it on the pages of the newspaper in disasters large and small, we see it in the countless small tragedies that from time to time overshadow us or the lives of those we love.

A while ago, and hauntingly, I remember seeing it in the eyes of two other pregnant unmarried children, the New Jersey college students Brian Peterson and Amy Grossberg, when they were arraigned for causing the death of their infant son. There was no room in their lives for a child . . . no room for a less than perfect story, no room for a humanity that admits of the possibility of humiliation or brokenness. There was no room in the inn this time for a god who might be born in the heart of trouble. And now that the angel has departed, what hovers over those once glorious young lives is grief, and terror, and unending sorrow and regret. The shadow of death has blotted out all the details of the grace and beauty that once were Amy and Brian's carefree lives—and where will they, or we, turn now, for a word of hope or a chance of good news?

When the other girl, the virgin Mary, ended *her* flight under the shadow, there was a burden of illegitimacy and the probability of disaster in her life looming large, larger than her hope of glory in the moment of Gabriel's singing ever had done. The angel would not return, so now Mary's burden and Mary's glory must be shaped—like God's son is to be shaped—by merely human hands.

Out of the fog and the fear and the confusion, a door opens, and Elizabeth's hand reaches out to draw Mary in, to comfort and to bless. *Blessed are you among women!* she says, and the baby she is to bear in her old age jumps for joy. Wise Elizabeth, who knows that no one can subsist on a diet of occasional glory. Wise woman, who senses that when our paths have been crossed by the glory of God or by the power of the shadow, we must be held by human hands, if we are to bear it and bring it home.

Lovely Elizabeth, who wears the wisdom of her years and carries also within her body a child of miracle, understands, and enters into the shadow, molding Mary's world with compassion and grace. What is the difference—between the shadow of death, and the shadow of glory?

What is the difference that permits the god to be born in the heart and life of one young girl, when only death is born in the other? What is the difference between those who are magnified and those who are destroyed? When the girl Mary sang of her pregnancy, *my soul magnifies the Lord*, she was saying, to translate it another way, my soul is *enlarged*. That is to say, in the lives of some people, the experience of disaster does not cause a destruction of the soul, but rather, provides a way that the soul can be enlarged and stretched. Or as author and teacher Joseph Campbell describes it: in certain situations, people's animal instincts and the higher instincts struggle together in our hearts. When the higher self wins, that is a virgin birth: a time in which the life of God can be born within us, incarnate again in the world.

That is what happened to Mary. She was no one particularly gifted, particularly special. Yet when the shadow loomed over her life, and there were choices to be made, whether for life or for death, Mary chose life . . . and as she chose it, glory won out over fear, and she was enlarged. Just as she swelled in pregnancy to give room to the holy child she carried, so her hope, her spirit, and her soul were enlarged by God. She was, quite simply, stretched beyond herself, filled past capacity by the bearing of God's good news. And she saw that it was within her hands and her power, whether to shut down or to enlarge the possibility of God's saving presence in the world.

We all have this choice. And it happens every day, that people face their choices and allow the glorious Christ to be born anew into a life over which the shadow has loomed. I received a few days ago in the mail a Christmas letter from a friend whose struggle with Parkinson's disease has become, according to her family, quite debilitating and serious. But you can't tell from her letter. *Mother is moving in with me*, the letter says, *so that we can be company for each other now that the children are gone*. And, *I am finally putting my ideas of starting a publishing company into action!*

Where someone else might speak with bitterness of a life shrunken by the reality of a difficult progressive disease, this glorious soul is enlarged, giving birth again to the God of hope who enlarges our souls, in order that we, in turn, might magnify that Holy Presence in the world.

Sometimes, when glory overshadows us—or sometimes, when the angel departs, leaving us alone and shadowed by trouble and possibilities less glorious—sometimes, when we know we have been visited by that presence but falter in the twilight with the responsibility of it all; sometimes human hands reach out to comfort and to bless, and we are saved. A woman, a man, a child, faces the shadow and turns toward the light, and room is made at the inn for the god to be born again. Luke knew this, and thus brought Holy Light into the body of a girl and the darkness of a stable. Elizabeth knew this; she who bore her own holy child in the silence of her husband's house and in the shadow of his vision. The Angel of God knew this, who came not to one of the mighty, but to a poor girl, an ordinary girl. Mary knew it; and in coming to know it, found that glory and humanity can be woven together, even in the body of a girl. And knowing it, she lifted up her voice and sang, *my soul magnifies the Lord, and my spirit rejoices in God my savior!* even though the angel had departed.

For when Mary and her cousin met in the hill country to pick up the pieces of a broken life, the glory was still there, sifted and shaded in human, homely hands. *Be not afraid*—Brian and Amy, and your little lost child; Mary and Joseph, and all the children of your heritage down through the ages; child of God and your parents on this glad baptismal day: *be not afraid*. The Mighty One who did great things for Mary will do the same for us, so we might all come to bear in our bodies the incarnate Christ—that wherever we are may become a holy place, enlarging our souls and blessing others with the shadow of glory, the living presence of God.

Merry Christmas, Amen.

Tuning My Heart

CHRISTMASTIDE

Isaiah 60:1–6   John 14

Birth Pangs

This sermon was preached on January 2, 2005, on the seventh day following the catastrophic Christmas tsunami that struck Indonesia, killing over 120,000.

On Thursday morning, I felt compelled to put away my Christmas things early, turning my attention away from a fading vision of the child in the manger and reluctantly toward the new year that was surging in on a tide of wreckage and death, of grief and the deepening pain of unanswerable questions about the way God is being in the world. I have turned off the news in favor of a last attempt at Christmas carols, and begin my work. The tree goes first. Next, one by one, I gently fold the pieces of my nativity scenes into tissue paper, organize them by country and type, and carefully replace them in their neatly labeled boxes. One, I notice is from India. The next, one I had bought from SERRV International—an organization devoted to fair trade for economically developing countries—just two weeks prior, from Indonesia. The last is from Sri Lanka. It is a puzzle, with colorful pieces and joyful tidings of good news to all people fit neatly, perfectly in place in a way, I think, they will never fit again. I look at the crèches one last time and wonder whether those who crafted them are still alive, or among those who have been swept away by the Christmas tsunami. I imagine the shepherds, the animals, the Marys and the Josephs, and even the baby Jesus, mud-spattered and broken, tossed in a pile, a holy jumble of lost souls for whom there will be no room in the inn for a long, long time....

Because of an unusual convergence of personal and global disasters in these past, last, darker-than-usual days of Advent and Christmas, I have been asked more frequently than I'm used to—and more pointedly than I feel comfortable with—just who in the hell I think this God is who would permit such things to happen: without warning, without vengeance, without a reason *why*? I have been asked, by people in pain who deserve to know, *what is God up to, anyway, and what good is God if he cannot prevent such catastrophes or protect his children?* And I do not guess that I have a particularly satisfying answer—not for myself—nor, I imagine, for those of you who have been asking. These terrible things are happening, and God is either willing it or allowing it—if, indeed we subscribe to a view of God as all-powerful, all-knowing. And if we do not, then, we are left with a God—or something less than god?—who cannot stop catastrophe or evil, who is powerless to prevent creation's—our—suffering.

Friday afternoon, a friend said to me—*sometimes you seem comfortable, maybe even glib about this "powerless God." Is it really that easy?* And I have to say—no, it's not. It's not easy to have no answer to the suffering of people I love, or for the groaning of creation and the world's children. It is heart wrenching to look at the deaths of two hundred thousand people, to pray about it, and to have no reasons, no miracles, no excuses. It's painful to hear the anger and the bewilderment and to have nothing much to offer but silence, compassion, and companionship . . . and more painful still to be a spokesperson for a God who seems to be offering only somewhat more of the same. We want God to keep bad things from happening to good people. And we want a God who stops good things from happening to bad people. And we are stuck with a God who does little of either, a God who, our most sacred story tells us, didn't even stop evil people from killing his own son. And choosing to continue to worship this God is not the easiest of choices.

But when we choose to live a life in relationship to the Divine Source, when we choose to follow the Christ who urged us to know the truth, so that it can set us free, we don't get the God we invented, who would be perfect, powerful, rewarding good and punishing evil, blessing and protecting us no matter what comes. We do not get an omnipotent fantasy with a big plan.

But, perhaps, if we are brave, we may have a relationship with a God who is true, and who is being revealed in the world, and in our lives, sometimes beautifully, but more often through what Isaiah called *the thick darkness*. A relationship in which holy moments—of seeing, or knowing, or being with God—break upon us like a flash of light in darkness. *You shall know the truth*, and the truth shall set us free. Free from the plastic perfection of the god of our childhood fantasies, and free for a life of partnership with the source of life that is through us, bringing creation to birth. The Word becomes flesh, and dwells among us. And is us. We worship a God who has made us free, and whose freedom to BE God—is consequently limited by how we are choosing to be human, and made in God's image.

It is clear that such freedom comes at a price—a price that we, and, I believe, even God is paying. Part of the price is that we have to continually think and re-think our ideas about the sovereignty of God, the power of God. Rather than being like the child who finds comfort and protection in the arms of a powerful and loving father, we have to endure the sadness of coming of age, of learning to love a parent who is neither perfect nor omnipotent, and whose love, however unconditional, cannot shield us from disaster or grief. If we are going to be as we were created to be, God's free children, we need to put on our big-girl pants and take our place as adults, co-creators. Sure, the world isn't being run the way we would have run it. But we're not running it. And we don't really know what "running it" entails, if we were to be honest. All we can do is choose to accept our part in it, or not. Choose to be brave enough to give up our script and wait in the darkness while we learn the truth and how to be free, or stubbornly stick to our old script, and give up our shot at the living God.

And as Jesus also said, *you know the way to the place where I am going.*

What is the way? When do we see you, God? When do we get to learn who you are? You already know what you are supposed to do to get there: love God, and love your neighbor. We can be a part of the nativity, of the birthing process, groaning with God, bringing something to life even though we can scarcely bear the pain or look at the blood or imagine how such a process could ever bring forth the miracle of a living child; or we can leave the room, and let life belong to others. The preacher and writer Barbara Brown Taylor tells a story about a cartoon someone gave her one time: a caricature of a street corner preacher, a sign hung round his neck that said, *the world is not coming to an end; therefore you must suffer along and learn to cope.*[15]

I was thinking about learning to cope, and how we do it, as I was presiding over the marriage of two members of our church family this past Monday. The groom had asked for "a sermon," and so I was telling them that marriage isn't easy . . . and even coming to a longed-for marriage with the dearest of friends does not protect a person or couple from suffering or disappointment. Relationships that matter—with a spouse, with a friend, with God—take a great deal of hard work and only unfold into

---

15. Taylor, *God in Pain*, 85–86.

fullness of joy when the partners in them embrace the fullness of truth as they learn it from the love of friends, from the experience of suffering and brokenness, from working against injustice, from walking alongside those who are trying to survive and thrive in this life, from ordinary, repetitive choices of living in faith and in fidelity with God and with each other and with the world. And I remember thinking how lovely it would be if our vows and our prayers and our support would shield those we love from hurt and disappointment—but it is not so.

And so we do the best we can; we live in community, and we bring the not inconsiderable power of our love for each other and for God and for the work of healing and good in this world to bear, together with all the hope we have, to help God guide a good creation through the dark channels and the bitter pangs of birth into a life worth living. And we cover each other over with the canopy of that power, as members of this community did last Monday when they raised a prayer shawl over the newlyweds as we blessed them into their new life together.

This is the *tallis*, the prayer shawl that I used that day. It was bought for me by my parents when they visited Israel, after I had visited Israel myself and witnessed a part of a bar mitzvah ceremony held atop a dry stone mesa overlooking the Dead Sea. Prayer shawls are given by parents to bar and bat mitzvahs as a sign that the children are ready to become adults in their faith. This ceremony took place in the red dirt fragments of the yeshiva that was the school for the Masada community, which in 74 CE committed suicide *en masse*, waiting for God's supernatural intervention while the Romans overran their mountain fortress. I thought it a depressing place to celebrate the beginning of an adult life of faith, that sad and windswept ruin where faith died unanswered almost two thousand years ago. But the rabbi said:

> *here, where a community died, and with it, the hopes of a dying nation, you take up the heritage of an old and profound faith. We do not know what life will bring you. We do not know what tomorrow holds. We do know that here, now, you are covered over by the sheltering canopy of family and friends, you have been given a faith and a story. Know who you are, and what you believe. Be ready, for our future is in your hands.*[16]

---

16. Paraphrased by author.

At the beginning of this New Year, the future of the world looks hard. And, it is in our hands, and we are in each other's, loving God and neighbor, and bringing the world to birth, together with the truth that is setting us free. Let us observe moments of silence for those who have been lost, and for what we all have lost, and for the work of beginning again to find shelter, a way home.

And then let us pray, in the words of a collect from the old prayer book:

> *Eternal God, who commits to us the swift and solemn trust of life; since we do not know what a day may bring forth, but only that the hour for serving you is always present, may we wake to the instant claims of your holy will, not waiting for tomorrow, but yielding today. Amen.*[17]

---

17. As quoted in Taylor, *God in Pain*, 86.

3

Hints of Dreams

Epiphany to Transfiguration Sunday

There is a temptation among parish ministers, I think, to view the Sundays between the end of Christmastide and the beginning of Lent as a kind of theological time-out, a homiletical hiatus for the preacher who, having just finished the high festival work of Advent and Christmas, might be catching her or his breath prior to undertaking the heavy lifting of the Lent-Easter cycle. The variability of the season—anywhere from four to nine Sundays, depending on Easter—mitigates against any tendency to "settle in" to a prolonged treatment of certain themes; and it is tempting to sail along on the ordinary time breezes of this in-between time with a weather eye turned toward the harder labor that Lent's forecast—*solemn reflection dead ahead*—seems to demand. The lectionary assignments for this season are driven in general by the gospel readings and their general themes of the early teaching ministry of Jesus. But the themes of the season scarcely seem to settle on one idea—the call of the disciples, perhaps, or a pairing of prophetic texts from Isaiah—before we are drawn without explanation or apology over toward the prophet Micah, or Jonah, or even into Deuteronomy. Still, there is gold here, and we are gifted in this season as once, long ago, the magi brought precious gifts to the child Jesus.

The feasts of the Epiphany and the Transfiguration, standing on either side of the beginning of Ordinary Time, gleam like beacons that link a strand of smaller lights twinkling bravely here and there throughout the still-long nights; they are the "Sundays after . . ." that illuminate the way along the path of ordinary considerations and practices of the people of God. It is wintertime still: Christmas is over, but the days are still short, and for some, cold and gloomy. It's not easy to be people of the Light, picking our way carefully between the possibilities and the perils of our calling. Like the magi who came from distant lands, our own journey through this in-between season is a work born more of uncertainty, from hints of dreams, than of glory.

Like the magi, like Jesus calling his disciples, like Eli or Samuel, Isaiah or even the reluctant Jonah—we are drawn from safer worlds and more familiar ways to wonder that God seeks folk such as we are, that God has visited and hallowed our earthy, fragile frames, embedded Light in the hard dull world like a jewel hidden in sullen, obscuring stone. We are magi, wise ones bidden to follow the Light and see where the child lies today, in us and in our world. What has God done? What are we to do?

Now that God hallows human flesh again, there is Light in us, Holy Light in all who are called by Jesus to be his folk in the world. Baptized like he was, into a new way of repentance and proclamation of the coming reign of God, we must be about uncovering that Light where it has been extinguished by the works of evil, or lain hidden in us, dimmed by our own faltering choices; so that, as Jesus taught, we might shine as a city set upon a hill. It is no accident that the Sunday of Transfiguration ends this season: a moment of glory, fleeting and poignant, to remind us what presence was wedded once to the peasant flesh of Jesus, the carpenter from Nazareth, and what high calling beckons us still, at Christ's invitation, *the one who believes in me will do the works that I do, and greater works than these.*[1]

I remember a story someone told me, about one of the old rabbinic masters, who was walking one day down a road with his students, debating the particulars of the turning of night to day. *Rabbi,* said one, *tell us when it is appointed that the night has ended, and the new day begun?* And the rabbi turned to his students and urged them, saying, *when, do you think, is the time that night turns to day?* And one ventured, *is it when you can stretch out your arm before you in the darkness and see your hand?* And the rabbi was silent for a time, lost in thought, and then spoke quietly to them all: *No, it is when there is enough light in you that you can look into the face of a stranger who passes you on the way, and recognize that one as your brother or your sister. When you can do that, you know that the night is ended, and the day has come.*[2]

---

1. John 14:12, NRSV.

2. The story is an adaptation of an adaptation of an adaptation. The source is a story by Rabbi Yitzchak Meir Rothenberg Alter (1799–1866) also known as the Chiddushei HaRim and the Rabbi of Ger. His teachings were translated from the Hebrew to the English by Martin Buber in: Tales of the Hasidim: The Later Masters, Schocken Book,

Hints of Dreams

THE FEAST OF EPIPHANY

January 6 *Matthew 2:1–12*

Seeking Stars

Here is a tale of those who would be wise, seeking stars: last fall, I taught a preaching course at the seminary in downtown Miami—it was a small group of men from competing religious traditions and widely differing cultural backgrounds. I was trying to find a way, one evening, to communicate how important it is for the preacher to gather from the common "stuff" of life, and to share with those who came to listen, something of what marks the presence of God in our lives—something of what helps us know that the Holy is really incarnate among us, as the promises of Christmas tell us. It was hard going: they were unsure of what I meant and kept trying to tell me explicitly religious stories, bible stories, theological precepts—things that, to them, were what "holiness" had to be all about. Finally, one of the men sat up a little straighter in his seat and spoke abruptly:

> *Wait, I get it, listen, I want to tell you all a story. There's this church in the Keys—a small, shabby looking Catholic church that I used to attend regularly. The furnishings were old and musty, and the people were kind of non-descript. There was this priest. He would come to Mass in the morning wearing shorts and a shirt, and sandals. He was a fisherman, and a very casual person. When he robed, you could see his hairy legs and feet, still in sandals, sticking out from beneath his alb. It was weird. But when he began the Mass something happened. There was this radiance around him . . . there was this connection with the earth and the island and the sea that made that room come alive, as he began to lead worship. The people all knew it—and whatever it was, it happened to them, to us all, as well—every time . . . I can't explain it, just—he was a fishing priest, and we could tell.*

As my student told it, his face aglow as though reflecting a light none of us could see, something happened to my small, disparate group, as well—something that pulled them up in *their* seats, drew them together

---

New York, 1948, page 308. The specific text is a comment on Exodus 10:23. It reads,
 The Darkness of the Soul: Concerning the passage in the Scriptures which deal with the thick darkness in the land of Egypt, where "they saw not every man his brother, neither rose any from his place," the rabbi of Ger said: "He who does not want to look at his brother soon gets to the point where he cleaves to his place and is not able to move from it."

and forward as one of them asked eagerly—*is it still like that? Could we go see it, too?* And the light died from his eyes—like that—as he said flatly, no. *No, you can't. It's gone now*—he moved away, and the bishop hired a non-fishing priest.

Here, too, is Matthew's tale of *wise men from the east*. Some of the translations, now, say, "astrologers" or "magi." Legend names them Caspar, Melchior, and Balthazar. Commentaries say that the three represent, perhaps, the great settled continents of the ancient world, all of which were called to pay homage and join the way of Jesus of Nazareth, the Christ. I say—this tale of the wise, however it came to be, is our story—it is why we listen, rapt, when we hear in another's voice or see reflected in another's face that fleeting, unmistakable touch of the Holy. Why we yearn for it, soul and body—and why, even if we do not know, precisely, what a "fishing priest" might be about, or a child, perhaps, who embodies the very presence of God—still, we long for it. And we would set out on that journey, if we only knew how and where to go. The story invites us to see how the magi came from the east, because they, too, wanted something more than what they had, something different.

They saw a star in the sky, and they knew that something holy, something wise, something real was being born into all the weary world. And because they were wise, they did not file that knowledge away as something interesting to tell on a dull evening, or disregard it as irrelevant to the working of the ways of the world, but hallowed it.

They saw a star, I say, and immediately all that mattered in their important and busy lives took a back seat to the necessity of seeking that star, and honoring whatever was at the end of that journey. They may have been important and busy people: but wise enough to know that there is nothing more important in our lives than the appearance of the Holy. So the wise left their busy and important lives behind, and they prepared gifts of precious things—gold, and frankincense, and myrrh. Then, gifts in hand and eyes searching the sky for signs, they set their feet on a journey toward the star, and they did not look back.

The Scriptures tell us to reverence such journeys—to take such journeys seriously—because they lead us to the transformation of life. But the Gospel of Matthew also tells us to proceed with caution—because we live in a world where such journeys are received with suspicion, with hostility, and with fear. *When king Herod heard all this, he was frightened.*[3] The story tells us that the world, and all the powers in it, will not gladly suffer us to leave our business and our common sense behind and to come, bearing gifts to a stranger. It will remind us, insistently, that we owe allegiance to darker, older sources. The world, Herod will tell us, is run by power, and by profit, and not by the light of a star—and woe be to anyone who forgets that reality or neglects to feed that relentless fire.

Truth to be told, sometimes it's hard to see the difference between the two—between following the star and feeding the fire of the world as it is. In the beginning, even the magi thought they could do both. They were on the way to see the child, following the star: but they thought it good to stop along the way and pay homage to that other king, Herod. Why would they not? It was the appropriate, the seemly, the prudent thing to do. And they had no reason to suspect, did they?—not any more than we usually do, that the power of the child and the power of the world were incompatible. In their innocence and their wisdom, they believed that any power that was would want to seek the star and worship the child, the newborn king along with them.

But we know differently—we who struggle always to balance the necessary with the Holy in our lives. We who watch what the world has done, down through the ages, to the ones who set the necessary in their lives aside to follow the star—the Martin Luther Kings, the Itzhak Rabins, the Jean d'Arcs. We know, as Matthew knew, that the will of the Herods of the world is always bent on the child's destruction; for the life of the child threatens the way of the world—*the way that says every man for himself* and *profit is the bottom line*. There is a certain wariness and caution and prudence that follows us, as we make our way in the world . . . a Herod-like knowledge that causes us, as soon as we have heard of a miracle child, a "fishing priest," a possibility of whatever kind that would bring the Holy among us once more—to lower our eyes, to still the sudden welling-up of hope, to slow our step and remember that the world does not honor those who seek stars.

Herod knows our cynicism and our wariness, and understands our weariness as well. Herod knew it would be easier to go along with the system than to fight it: and knowing it, he called the magi, and beguiled them with reasonable words, expecting that the habit of obedience to power

---

3. Matthew 2:3, NRSV.

would bring them back, or that the possibility of co-opting their vision would dull its wild edges. Herod called them in secrecy, and hoped that his offers would outweigh the loveliness of the dream and the light of the star; but it was not to be. For those who have seen the light of the star, and worshipped God at the cradle of the Holy Child, cannot easily resume their old habits and their indifferent ways.

It was the light of the star that called a small fellowship of black and white police officers in West Miami-Dade to keep knocking at the door of a certain Denny's restaurant; to push the point and push it until it was clear that it *was* their very fellowship—the color-blind fellowship of the wise—that had caused the doors to be locked against them in the first place. It was the light of that star that made it more important to pursue justice than to bow to the common knowledge that racism is part of the way things are, part of the realm of Herod. It would have been easier to walk away: *what would it matter, really, when there are hundreds more restaurants, so little time, and fighting is such a hassle?* But those who know the light of the star cannot go along with the way things are—because they have been changed by that journey, and they cannot go back—they must go home, as the magi did, by a different way.

Herod has had—oh, he will have—his day. But this is the season of Epiphany, the time of the star's appearing, and the power of Herod has no place here. And that is the mystery of the magi: they were star-seekers, dreamers of dreams—and still, with the power of Herod arrayed against them, they came in safety to worship the child, and went home—never again to be the same—by another way.

What would it be like for us, for each of us, to be numbered among the wise? Not to reserve our star-seeking for church, or to look for signs only when we are planning to take time out for the holy, but instead, to make it a very part of who we are, woven into the fabric of our being?

On the Wednesday before Epiphany, at a study group where several of us talked about the congregation's upcoming celebration of Old Christmas, one person mentioned that she wanted to bring a gift, but could not think of a Christmas story or poem she could share. *But it doesn't have to be a Christmas story,* I said, *any kind of a story is a gift.* And I thought: *how easy it is for us to lay aside our search for the star, our seeking for meaning, our attempts to make justice and build community, and to reserve them only for Christmastime, holy times.* It is like the fact that, the last Friday of every month for a year, five or six or eight folks from our church have pulled themselves away from work and home and weekend plans to trek downtown to serve dinner at the Homeless Assistance shelter, because no one else wanted to give up a Friday night. But the Friday after Christmas, when we went down, there were twenty people crammed into that little space, eager to show a Christmas charity on that day that, the rest of the year, perhaps, went wanting. It is so difficult for us to carry our gifts with us for all seasons, to show attentiveness to the presence of the holy in our common stories, to practice an everyday devotion to the work of the Christmas Christ; it is so hard not to forget who we were made to be, when we were made star seekers.

We are fishing priests, all of us, walking on holy ground with hairy legs and sandaled feet. Finding amidst the ordinary and the boring and the drab, the promise of light and the presence of the holy. Taking time to do it . . . and then to go home, back to our ordinary lives, always changed, ever renewed.

I saw my former student at an Epiphany party this year, and I asked him, *remember that story you told us? Whatever happened to your parish after the non-fishing priest came?* And the man grinned as he said,

> *A while ago, the bishop came down to the Keys for a little relaxation. He stopped in at Mass, and afterwards took the new priest aside and said, "hey, I'm here in the Keys for two more days. Can you take me fishing tomorrow?" And the priest said, shocked, "But, sir, we can't go fishing! Tomorrow is a Holy Day of Obligation." And they were both quiet for a minute. Then the bishop looked at the priest with great seriousness and authority and intoned "Holy Mackerel." They went fishing.*

And so may we, in all seasons. Amen.

Tuning My Heart

THE SEASON OF EPIPHANY
THE BAPTISM OF THE LORD

Mark 1:1–11

The Birthday of Martin Luther King Jr.

A Place to Begin

Just once, try starting this way: a sermon, a story, a speech, a conversation. With no explanation, no excuses. No embellishment, no set up. No story to help us understand, to make it pretty, to soften the rough edges and give people a chance to get warmed up. Just twelve terse words that mean everything—and then, silence—before you have even realized what it is you are about to hear: *the beginning of the gospel of Jesus Christ, the son of God.*

It is a strange place to start—why then? Why there? Why those people, and not the others? Where are the magnificent angels, the picturesque shepherds? The long ride to Bethlehem, the humble, obedient virgin and her faithful husband? Where are the wise men, the stars, the portents in the heavens? What happened to the long, lovely story, with the music that starts right after Halloween so that there can be no chance that you might miss the beginning of the show?

One summer in the mountains of Colorado, my family went out to watch the Persiad meteor shower, which happens annually in August. We did everything we could to prepare. We knew what we were looking for, and we knew what time to look. We spent the long summer day staking out different viewing sites, then packed our blankets and snacks, and waited for darkness to fall. From the best vantage point, we laid flat on our backs in the big darkness of a western Colorado wilderness night, positioned ourselves for maximum exposure . . . and waited. *There! Quick! Over here! No, down there!* If your head was turned even a little bit, you missed it. As soon as one of us could see it, it was gone, a flash in the darkness, a fading streak across the night sky, a memory of something not-quite-seen. And that is how it is with the Gospel of Mark: not knowing where to look, he picks a point in the sky, a flash of the heart, and goes with it: *the beginning of the gospel of Jesus Christ, the son of God.*[4] And everything unfolds from *that* place, *that* solitary moment of choosing.

Sometimes I imagine the writer of Mark's Gospel, trying to begin: *once upon a time*—no. *When Jesus was born in Bethlehem of Judea*—no. *When Jesus was a small boy in Nazareth*—no. *In the beginning was the Word*—no, no, no. None of those would do, all of those went back too far, started far too carefully for the urgency Mark's writer felt to communicate the beginning of the changing of his world. Finally with a heap of parchment on the floor, and the frustration of a word that simply needed to be told, Mark chose simply to *begin* . . .

And I do not believe it was entirely by accident that the place Mark chose was the baptism of Jesus in the wilderness . . . for it is a story of another man—like Mark, maybe, and maybe even a bit like us, who lived his life and marked his years until one day, it was time to begin.

This is the beginning of the gospel of Jesus Christ, the Son of God. A man named Jesus, from the backwater village of Nazareth of Galilee, walked down from his home one day to seek out a stranger in the wilderness near the Jordan River. He was not a young man by the standards of his time, yet the story stubbornly refuses to tell us what he had been doing with his life up until that moment; why he had come to that place at that time; or whether he even knew what he was about when he walked down into the waters, the uncharted waters of his baptism.

He just appeared, unnoticed and unremarkable, and it seems to me quite possible that *this* gospel writer expects us to believe that Jesus had no idea who he was . . . just that somehow, he needed to get down to the Jordan that day and prepare himself for—who knew what? Without angels, shepherds, stars, or magi, with no mysterious birth, no mother keeping and pondering the meaning of miracle, the Jesus of the Gospel of Mark was just another ordinary Jewish man—another face in the crowd, with nowhere particularly special to go and not much reason to be missed if somehow, he never get there.

In the Gospel of Mark, no one seems to expect much of Jesus, no one seems to know who he is, no one even once calls him the "Son of God"—except the demons—until that last day, at the bitter end of his life, when a foreigner he had never met, a Roman centurion, looked up at the dying Jewish criminal and murmured in awe: surely this man was a Son

---

4. Mark 1:1, NRSV.

of God. In the Gospel of Mark, even John, the baptizing one, did not know who he was, might even have missed him in the crowd, for all we know.

But we know: Jesus was baptized by John in the Jordan, and when he came up out of those uncharted waters, something happened. John did not see it, the crowd did not hear a thing, but Jesus did.

He heard a voice, he saw a shattering vision of heaven being ripped in two (just as, much later, the temple's curtain would be ripped in two at the moment of his death)—he saw heaven open and the spirit of God brooding over him, God's new creation . . . and in that moment of startling vision, Jesus began to understand, perhaps for the first time: he was chosen, set apart. He was God's own child, called to do God's work, that moment and forever.

And what did that mean? Did that mean that Jesus, more enviably than most of us, came up out of the waters of his baptism with supernatural clarity and magnificent purpose, a life map writ in the stars? I am not sure—but I do not think so. I think Jesus may have come up out of his baptism much like we come up out of ours—mostly wet, but somehow prompted to understand that, whatever it might be that we are going to end up in the middle of—God will somehow be there in the middle with us.

Where does your story of the gospel begin? What is the beginning of the gospel—the good news of how you are God's child in God's right place and time? Can you remember? Can you claim it? Or, if you cannot, will you find a place to begin, here, now—even if it is virtually in the middle of the story, as it was for Mark? The point is, to begin.

If Mark's Jesus did not need angels, a miraculous birth, a star or wise men . . . your story of the gospel does not either. If Mark's Jesus did not always know who he was and where he was going—but found his vocation, his calling, at the right moment, prompted by his circumstances, John's preaching, whatever it was in that God-moment combination of word and water and sky and air—so can you. When does the gospel of your life begin?

Choosing a place is not a matter of right or wrong, but a matter of listening for God, and paying attention to the promptings that call one thing to your attention, awakening your passion, rather than some other. For the Gospel of John it was in the beginning was the Word; for Luke, now in those days a decree went out from Caesar Augustus; neither is right, neither is wrong, each are real ways of telling the beginning of the gospel of Jesus Christ. There is no right place to begin for everyone . . . but there is a right place to begin for you.

One of the privileges, the blessings, of being church together is the chance we have to witness such beginnings. To note them, to celebrate them, to stand shoulder to shoulder with one another during the birth pangs of the gospel as it is born in us. Not to have our stories flash by, like a shooting star, a brief point of light in the darkness, missed because no one was looking the right way—but to have such moments witnessed, oohhed and ahhed over—like the gift of God each story, each beginning, surely is.

Each star, each story, begins in a different place—appropriate to its teller, shaped in the holy constellation of one soul's path shining forth in the galaxy of the communion of saints. Two months ago, during a peace-prayer service in the congregation I serve in Miami, I witnessed one such beginning, when a woman in her mid-fifties stood up in the middle of church, and said, I was raised an Episcopalian, have been a Christian all my life, but only now, as I have discovered within myself a passion for Christ's work of peace, do I understand what it is to be the child of God. And she wept as she described what it meant for her to stand in the middle of U.S. Highway 1 each Friday afternoon and wave signs against the war in Iraq, what it meant for this sometime coffee-kiosk owner and part-time office manager to find her vocation, her work as a child of God. And the church wept too, for they knew: it was the beginning of the gospel of Sarah.

In 1968, the day after Martin Luther King Jr. was assassinated, a public school teacher in Riceville, Iowa, found the beginning of her gospel in the eyes of her stunned, all-white, third grade class. Why did they shoot that king? said one small boy, and their teacher knew she had to do something she had been wanting to try for years. Breaking up her little class according to their eye color, Mrs. Jane Elliott instituted a week of discrimination. Children wore colored collars to set one group apart from the other. Blue eyes were forbidden to use the water fountain one day, and ridiculed for wastefulness when they threw away a paper cup. Brown eyes were told that all brown-eyed parents spanked their children, and were lazy and useless. Children of different colors were forbidden to play with one another. By the second day, anxiety and aggression had filled the eyes of a class divided—children who were formerly cooperative, cheerful, and companionable. A brown-eyed boy punched his blue-eyed friend on the playground. Asked why, he said, his voice dropping in shame, "because he called me a bad name—he called me "brown-eyed."

On the last day, Mrs. Elliott ended eye color separation. She asked the kids how it felt, and told them they could do whatever they liked with their collars. In a moment, collars were torn from small necks, ripped into shreds by small teeth, and trampled in the garbage. Freed from artificial divisions, they opined that racism was "stupid." Was it the end of the story of Martin Luther King Jr.? No, rather it was the beginning of the gospel for thirty little blue- and brown-eyed kids who learned that color does not separate . . . and the beginning of the gospel of Jane Elliott.

My young friends Jenny and Mark learned recently in the midst of a longed-for pregnancy that their unborn daughter would be affected—they did not know how severely—with Down syndrome.[5] They were told: you can choose—abort, or carry this fetus to term. They talked about it, they prayed. They learned what they could, they wept. They sat with their pastor; they shared with their family. They went away to make their decision in privacy, and then called me. We've made a decision. We want to talk to you about it. They did not think they had the will, the strength, to bring that child to life. They were not mature enough to sustain their marriage, their demanding professional lives, and a child with profound disabilities.

Their decision, a difficult and painful one, was compassionately supported by their friends, their family, and their church. But two hours before their appointment with me, they each had a dream, and then, a moment. Jenny had been praying for a "nudge" from the Spirit—some kind of clearer sign about which way to go. Mark arose from a nap, restless and exhausted, his resolve set: they just couldn't do it. He climbed into the shower, and as the water poured over his head, suddenly knew that, unless he chose another path, in his words, I will never become the man I am meant to be. Jenny looked at him, and saw: this was the nudge, the word from God: our "no" needs to be "yes." Honey, we're going to have this child, she said, and immediately peace fell over both of them. It was the beginning of the gospel of Jenny and Mark. When I saw them an hour later, I did not see a young couple in the throes of a life-challenging decision, I saw the faces of Christ.

And their daughter Amanda, child of promise, was baptized in the midst of an Advent season more holy than usual, and she was, I say, emmanuel, God with us. God is with us: and the good news of the gospel is: the gospel is, and it is now. Where does your Christ-story begin? When?

---

5. Jenny and Mark's names have been changed; the story is told with their permission.

Hints of Dreams

Pick a place—any place, and know: it is the beginning of the gospel of Jesus Chris—for you. Amen.

THE SEASON OF EPIPHANY

Isaiah 62:1–5   John 2:1–11

Insignificant Matters

And Jesus said, what concern is that to you and to me?
John 2:3

Last summer, on a hot, bright June afternoon, I finally got the opportunity to do something I had wanted to do for a long time—I walked up the steps and into the cool, holy darkness that is the Cathedral of St. John the Divine in Manhattan. I was not sure what I had been expecting, all those years—I had seen pictures, listened to organ concerts and symphonies that had been recorded in the echoing vault of the nave of the church—I had, one or two times, driven past the cathedral in a cab, craning my head out the window to see how the towers climbed on either side of the building—I had glimpses, and pieces—but no apprehension of the whole. I walked by the information desks, through the dark stained, massively carved doors. I heard my heels clicking across the slate floor, and the murmured hush of whispering tourists up somewhere behind the high altar. I walked to the middle of the sanctuary, and turned around to lift my eyes to the magnificent rose window floating above the balcony. Faint streaks of light etched their path through the window's colored pieces and slanted their way, full of dust, to the floor far below. *Holy*, echoed a memory in my mind, *holy, holy, holy, Lord God of hosts*. I realized that I was weeping, tears streaming down my face for minutes, in fact, but I couldn't say why.

In such a manner do we come to the surprising first sign of Jesus in the Gospel of John. We have been led, in the prologue to the gospel and even in the initial story of John the Baptist and his discovery of Jesus by the Jordan River, to expect something special, something holy, something so precious that it would defy description, bring us to tears. *Behold*, says John, *and you can hear the hush of awe in the words, behold the Lamb of God, who takes away the sins of the world!*[6] We have been waiting for such a very long time, preparing and reading the signs, craning our necks up toward heaven, hoping for a glimpse of it until, there it is—*the Word became flesh and dwelt among us, full of grace and truth. And we have beheld his glory, glory as of the only begotten Son of God.*[7] Here is no child born to an unmarried girl in the ignominy of a stable. No, here is the Word, the Logos, the Light: the being and the power and the glory of God, descended straight from heaven *that*, as the writer of the fourth Gospel says repeatedly, *we might believe that Jesus is the Christ, the son of God, and believing, have life in his name.*[8] And we are ready, feet ascending the long steps and hand poised to push open the heavy door, long past ready to behold *glory*, that we might be changed.

In the Gospel of John, the miracles—or as the fourth Gospel puts it, the "signs" of Jesus—are as infrequent as a cathedral visit, momentous, and sparingly used. In all of the whole gospel, there are only seven signs given—marked contrast to the supernatural generosity of the Synoptic Gospels accounts, where the miracle work of Jesus is frequently told. In the Gospel of John, the signs focus mostly on significant acts of restoration in the lives of individuals or in the life of the community: the healing of the lame man at the pool of Bethsaida, the raising of Lazarus from the dead, the multiplication of the loaves and fishes for the feeding of the hungry hoards longing for the Word of life from Jesus. The signs are usually matched with a discourse on the nature of Jesus and his work—how he is bread of Life, shepherd of the sheep, the true vine, the resurrection and the Life. Each of the signs is given for one purpose, and one purpose only: to reveal Jesus' glory, and to cause people to *believe, and, believing, have life in his name*. The signs have dignity, purpose, majesty, power. They are important, as Jesus himself is important.

Of all the signs, only the changing of water into wine at the wedding feast of Cana in Galilee seems, by contrast, to be a frivolous and insignificant demonstration of the Word made flesh. We have been expecting to find ourselves consumed by the holy, transported—but instead, we are

6. John 1:29, NRSV.
7. John 1:14, NRSV.
8. John 20:21, NRSV.

squeezed around a table, surrounded by smoke and noise, struggling to hear and see as the plates clatter and the last dregs of wine are tossed back by an already slightly inebriated hoard of unruly fellow guests. Of *holy, holy, holy!* there is nothing to be heard at all, not even a faint echo.

One wonders whether even Jesus himself was preoccupied by the notion that his ministry of signs would be entirely taken up with the numinous, the more obviously and ostentatiously holy, the wholly Other. Certainly it seems that Jesus had not anticipated that this homely, common event would have anything to say to him or to the world about who he was and what he was called to do.

There they are: Jesus, his disciples, his mother, and their friends. It is a wedding, and all have gathered for a celebration of the commonplace, the joining of a man and a woman in marriage. They were all eating, and drinking, and everything was as it should be, even down to one of those embarrassing and inexplicable disasters that seem to afflict and humanize events of this nature—*remember, the ring bearer swallowed the bride's band? The maid of honor passed out, right at the altar? The minister's cat walked straight up the aisle in the middle of the service? They ran out of wine at the reception?* It is the stuff of family memories, but hardly the habitat of the holy.

With a horrified whisper, the mother of Jesus was the first, apparently, to notice that another such wedding party crisis had ensued. The wedding feast had been, as was the custom, a long party, days long, in fact . . . and with more guests than had been anticipated. Everyone had a *very* good time . . . so good, in fact, that here, in the last hours of the feast, the casks of wine had given out, and there was nothing left to drink. It was not, as the world goes, a terrible disaster, but as the host reddened and gestured and servants went flying to the corners of the house, only to return empty-handed, there was one woman who paid attention to detail, whose heart was touched with a compassion of the commonplace, and who went immediately to the only person she could think of who might do anything about it. *Jesus! Psst! Son! Look, they've run out of wine. Do something!* And then, having done what she could, she waited.

But the Jesus of John's Gospel is not sure that this surpassingly ordinary household crisis has much to do with his mission and his call. He is meant, after all, for greater things—this Word made flesh, this Light from Light, this Savior to be, who is only now beginning his public ministry and surely knows how important it is that his first great act be just that—a great one. I see him, a young man dressed in clothes too new to be comfortable, dragged by his family to a wedding he would rather have missed; now drawn unwillingly into the public eye, irritated at his mother's stubborn insistence. *Be still, woman,* he hisses back. *What concern is this of yours or of mine? Quit pushing.* And then, somewhat self-importantly, perhaps hoping to quell her, *my hour has not yet come.*

But it had come, he just didn't know it yet. His hour had come—not the important one, not the hour of his sacrifice toward which, already, this young rabbi looked ahead with sorrow and weary determination. Not *that* hour, but *an* hour—an hour for recognizing that, even in the smallest and most insignificant of matters, there is a chance for the holy to be born, a way to gladden the hearts of people—even people who think their biggest problem is whether there will be enough food at the reception. It was a small concern—Jesus was right!—no great matter, and the world would not have stopped or begun again over whether there was wine enough for the party ... but in a way, Mary was right, too. For more often than we imagine, that which is insignificant *matters.*

For Mary, that ponderer of secrets, that observer of details, knew that holiness begins at home; and that those who would be holy, must first hallow the commonplace in their own lives, and cultivate it. The Jesus of John was set for a high and holy task, but it took a mother to remind him that the high and the holy must needs be rooted in honoring the simplest of things. Glory is revealed in the ordinary, even in the frivolous, gifts of life. And the first sign of John reminds us that if we are ever to recognize the holy at all, we must first cultivate it in our own back yards.

And so Jesus, Son of God, humbled himself by listening to the voice of a woman. He humbled himself to attend to the needs of a hoard of half-drunk neighbors, humbled himself to begin his own great journey with a small act of joy. He squandered his first of seven precious signs on a homely wedding party—and here's the punch line: almost no one noticed. Oh, they drank the wine, it's true. They marveled at its quality, called for more, had one last bite, made ribald jokes, but when at last they went their way, they were satisfied and happy but none the wiser.

And the story says, *Jesus did this, the first of his signs, in Cana of Galilee, and his disciples believed in him.*[9] Nobody but the disciples noticed;

---

9. John 2:11, NRSV.

but that is not a bad thing. For all celebrated—and the few who needed to know the difference, did. And, it is to be hoped, learned something from it that would change *their* own work . . . as Jesus learned from his mother something that changed *his*. There is glory in the most mundane thing we do, when we do it for love. There is holiness in the most insignificant of commonplace events—if we are disciples, and if we are looking for it. There is a high and a holy task for each of us . . . but more than likely, charity begins at home.

I need to learn this lesson, and learn it well—for I am one who goes always seeking that which is high and holy, as I once yearned for the dark and cool stones of the Cathedral of Saint John the Divine to carry me to a place in the spirit I had never been before. I do not want to be so carried away by the high way that I miss the changing of water into wine.

To that end, let me tell you a story of a woman of this church, who recently celebrated her hundredth birthday, and with whom, from time to time, I am privileged to celebrated the sacrament of Holy Communion. Ruth's hearing is not so good, and the fact that her two small dogs are yipping as we visit doesn't make it any easier for either of us to hear. We sit knee to knee, on spindly Victorian-era chairs, while her seventy-five-year-old daughter sits across the room, shushing the puppies. *JESUS TOOK BREAD! I shout, AND BROKE IT!!!* Ruth smiles serenely, and the puppies bark energetically. *THIS IS THE BODY OF CHRIST, BROKEN FOR YOU!!!* And we do break it.

The puppies, anticipating a snack, renew their barking, and begin attempting to jump over the barrier behind which they are confined. I take the cup—it is one of those small, shot glass affairs that come with home communion sets, and I continue, even louder, with the words of institution: *THIS IS THE CUP OF THE NEW COVENANT!!! DRINK YE ALL OF IT!!!* And it is hard to be holy, when you are shouting at the top of your lungs and hoping the dogs do not get loose. But the lady and her daughter lift their cups, as I lift mine, and just before I close my eyes to pray, they make that universally recognized gesture—*Bottoms up!* and toss back the grape juice in a shot. For a moment, I feel like I am at a very disorganized and chaotic party, and I am sure I have failed again to convey the holy during this important visit—but then, a bubble of laughter rises to my lips, and a certainty overtakes me: I *am* at a party—like a wedding feast of Cana in long-ago Galilee again—and there is wine, and a sign—and just for a second, the room is flooded with glory, and I, a disciple at last, believe.

Tuning My Heart

SEASON OF EPIPHANY

Jonah, Chapters 3 and 4

"Something Very Basic"

At a spontaneous memorial service for Rickia Isaac, a little girl whose life a random gunshot claimed recently in the city of Miami, Florida, a young mother spoke for all of us. Lebonah Israel told of the precautions she takes, in that difficult neighborhood, to protect her own two children. She described crack dealers, prostitutes, large dogs and home schooling. She listened attentively while yet another outraged, invaded community mourned the loss of a baby, and vowed we shall overcome. And then, looking at the reporter, she shook her head when she was asked whether she believed things would be different, after Rickia's death. *Maybe*, she said. *But I doubt it. Nothing can change until something very basic changes. Not until people start feeling love instead of hate and anger.*[10]

Here, I feel, is the point of the tale of Jonah, a short story that is a searching, biting commentary upon the racism that divides people and the hatreds that poison the human heart so that, as Lebonah Israel feared, nothing ever changes. Indeed, the last time this little book came up on the lectionary, we were at war with Saddam Hussein, and the nation of Israel was facing off against her Palestinian family and her Arab neighbors. This morning, what has changed?

In the Israel of the fifth century before the birth of Jesus, things were complicated. It was the time of the return of the Jewish people from exile—a time to celebrate a newly reconstituted nation, a time to affirm national identity. People who had maintained their religious and cultural integrity throughout seventy years of captivity were coming home in triumph to restore their heritage; those who had remained behind to keep the candles of Judah's faith dimly burning rejoiced with hope and energy renewed.

But things were complicated. Though many Jews had remained faithful in exile, others had not maintained standards. Some married out of the faith—the women of enemy tribes. Their children spoke no Hebrew, their heritage had been neglected. Though the Temple of Jerusalem had been rebuilt, its shabby and rustic appearance was a continual mockery of all that the people had lost, a bitter symbol of bygone glory. Natural disaster

---

10. Amy Driscoll, *Miami Herald*, January 25, 1997, p. 1B.

had created a situation of endemic poverty and widespread discontent. It was a difficult time—a time that needed vision, and unprecedented national unity. It was a time to celebrate us—and to reject them. Finally, a national consensus was built upon a politics of negativism, exclusivity, and hatred. The leadership of Judah, Nehemiah, and Ezra, forcibly broke up all mixed marriages. Foreign wives and their mestizo children were set aside. A strict policy of adherence to the religious codes of the Torah was demanded and enforced. And in time, the discipline paid off, and Israel rose again as a nation: strong, proud, at peace . . . but in rising thus, they paid a price.

Exclusivism bred prejudice and suspicion of others, creating a national consensus of hatred. Religious legalism and literalism squelched prophetic spontaneity, especially the lyrical visions of prophets like Second Isaiah, who had foreseen Israel not merely as a flame, a refiner's fire, but as a light to and for the Gentiles—those now-hated "Others." And in such times, then as now, alternative voices were not kindly heard.

But still they spoke—and in due course, their vision was placed side by side in the Bible with the sterner stuff of Ezra and Nehemiah. The book of Ruth reminded Israel that a foreign woman was a part of the ancestry of King David. The book of Esther, not even mentioning the name of God, demonstrated how the Divine could work powerfully for good even in the heart of a foreign court. And Jonah—well, the writer of Jonah reminded those who needed to hear that God's grace is never restricted to one small corner of the globe; and that even the enemies of the people of God are embraced within the astounding scope of the mercy and love of the Creator.

For Jonah, our reluctant hero, it was a lesson grudgingly learned. The story is set in a period of history when Israel was destroyed by the Assyrian nation—by the way, the land now occupied by the nation of Iraq. Commissioned to preach to that despised nation, Jonah, a righteous and God-fearing Israelite, is filled with horror and revulsion at his task. Assyrian power had brought Israel to her knees. Assyrian atrocities had deeply embittered the Jewish people. For hundreds of years following the fall of the Israelite nation, the name of Assyria and its capital city were the very expression of evil incarnate, the perpetrators of holocaust.

And the God who could not stand silent in the face of the suffering of his people spoke, and said, *go at once to Nineveh, that great city, and cry out against it, for their wickedness has come up before me.*[11] And Jonah went—the other way.

Called to travel overland to the limits of the civilized East, Johan hopped a ship and went West, as far as any soul could go. We all know the fish story that followed, the storm on the deep and the bed in the belly of a great fish; and how Jonah was compelled at last to answer his call, burped up on the shores that were the gateway to the great and terrible city of Nineveh. He would fulfill his call—and how.

Stalking a day's journey into the city, burning with rage and humiliation, with resentment and fear, Jonah found a likely spot, unpacked his striped tent, his sound system, the chairs, and the pulpit, and unrolled the sign across the tent poles: *Revival Tonight! Repent, for the Judgment of God is A-Comin'.* And then he waited. Darkness fell, and one by one the chairs, the benches, and the empty spaces between were filled. The sides of the tent were rolled up, and the people pressed in by the hundreds, and still they came. Men, women, children, cows, goats, and chickens—a restless sea of anxious faces ... until Jonah could bear it no more. Cranking up the sound system to its highest volume, the prophet whipped out his handkerchief, mopped his sweaty brow, raised his big black Bible in his clenched fist and roared: *Forty days more, and Nineveh shall be overthrown!*[12] Eight words, and what an opening line! Lord, did it feel good. He paused to gauge the effect of his words, and licked his lips in anticipation. Sucking in another great breath, he prepared to go on, but—wait, what was that? Before him in the tent, and for blocks around outside, one unexpected sound was arising—a great and heartbroken wail from the unified soul of the enemy: *we repent! Don't destroy us! We didn't know.*

Before Jonah's unbelieving eyes, an entire nation fell to its knees in sorrow and hope. Cattle and other beasts, men and women and children alike, tore their clothes, threw ashes over their heads, and prayed as they had never prayed before to a God that they had not known existed.

---

11. Jonah 1:2, NRSV.
12. Jonah 3:4, NRSV.

Hints of Dreams

And the hope of that enemy people in the heart of a God and not their own was a sobering and holy thing to behold: *all shall turn from their evil ways*, the king said, *Who knows? God may relent and change his mind* . . .[13]

And God did. And God did relent! And Jonah? Jonah stood dumbfounded in the midst of the empty tent, surveying the overturned chairs and the crumpled bulletins. A wind blew across his pulpit, and the fifteen unpreached pages of his manuscript of damnation scattered across the courtyard. Tears filled his eyes, and he bowed his own head in prayer. *Lord*, he began, *I knew this would happen*. And as bitterness filled his heart, he went on, almost spitting out the words, *I knew you were a God, rich in mercy, slow to anger, and abounding in steadfast love. I knew you would repent, and permit those disgusting people to live. I am the most successful revivalist in the history of the human race and I might as well be dead. What is life worth, after all, if there is no difference between us and them?*

Isn't that just like the Lord? And isn't Jonah just like us? Filled with gratitude at God's mercy toward us; filled with glee at God's judgment upon them. Preachers of love, but practitioners of division and hatred. Children who joyfully receive every shred of parental attention and compete for every gift, but begrudge with mathematical accuracy one tiny extra moment spent upon a brother or a sister. Ready to wail with outraged disappointment—*you always! You never! Why didn't you* . . . Aren't we like that, aren't we really? Just like the woman said, nothing will really change, until something very basic changes. And basically, things aren't too much different than in Jonah's time.

Leonard Pitts, a columnist for the *Miami Herald*, asks: *Can white apologize? Can black forgive?*[14] The new pastor of a neighboring Metropolitan Community Church, a predominately lesbian, gay, and bisexual congregation, phoned to ask: *are you doing anything ecumenical for Ash Wednesday and Lent? Could we participate? Would your clergy colleagues be uncomfortable?* And sure enough, one of our neighboring Presbyterian communities withdrew from our long-shared Ash Wednesday worship, saying sadly that they were sorry we had decided to invite "others" to participate, and they weren't comfortable meeting at the Table of Jesus Christ with "those people." An African American preacher with whom I shared the story of a friend's robbery in South Miami asked—*was she white?* And

---

13. Jonah 3:8–9, NRSV.
14. Leonard Pitts, *Miami Herald*, January 25, 1997.

to my shame, it was an hour before it even occurred to me that neither one of us—black pastor nor white pastor—even thought to question the racial identity of the two men who held her up—we just assumed—united in this sad way over the gulf that separates our races—that the robbers must have been black. Nothing very basic has changed—we have not changed, despite our efforts to the contrary—and so, the story is still the same. Not an eight word sermon like Jonah's this time, but three sad words that sum up the state of the human family: *us and them*. Can that be the end of the story?

No, it cannot, for after this tragedy of judgment deferred, God decides to plays with Jonah a little. Following him out into the back yard, God watches while Jonah plants himself in a patch of broiling sun, a picture of martyred misery. Like an amused but tender parent, God makes a leafy bush grow up, bringing blessed merciful shade to cover the sulking prophet. Jonah begins to relax—someone has at last noticed he's been done wrong—but then—poof! The bush withers and dies, and Jonah is broiling again in the sun, twice as angry as before.

God asks: *Is it right for you to be angry?* And Jonah's reply is still filled with self-righteous indignation: *yes, angry enough to die*.[15] And God replies—*you cared about the plant, which you did not work for and which you did not grow, which appeared overnight and perished overnight. And should not I care about Nineveh, that great city, in which there are more than a hundred and twenty thousand persons who do not know their right hand from their left, and many beasts as well?*[16]

It is the best last line in the Bible—and the hardest. *Should God not be concerned?* For God takes as given what we have despaired of, what we have forgotten—that something very basic can, should, and must change in the hearts of the children of God, so that the kingdom of God might indeed be near. Leonard Pitts put it this way, as he considered whether race relations in our country might be mended by the simple grace of repentance and forgiveness:

> *We ought to apologize, even to those who scorn the act. Forgive, even when brethren find it a cowardly response to horrific crimes. We ought to do these things not as a kindness to the other, but as an act of mercy to ourselves. Otherwise, these things hold us, and we, in turn, grip one another—unwilling to draw close, unable to let go—fastened together*

---

15. Jonah 4:9 NRSV.
16. Jonah 4:11, *TANAKH*, The Holy Scriptures.

Hints of Dreams

by the deeds of our fathers and the words left unsaid. The deeds are immutable, but the words await only courage.[17]

Amen, and amen.

SEASON OF EPIPHANY

Isaiah 6:1–13

Holy Roller Coaster

I love roller coasters now, but it was not always that way. When I was a little girl, our family went to the World's Fair site near New Orleans, I think, and I kept looking up at the lights of the highest ride, how they glittered and towered over the earth, a vision, *high and lifted up.* I wanted to be there in the worst way, but, I warned my father, *don't take me on any scary roller coaster rides, I hate them.* Hour by hour, we rode the lesser lights, and found them pleasant, but unmoving. I kept looking up, wondering and fearing. Finally my dad said: *let's try this one, it goes up to the top of the lights.* I asked him if it was the roller coaster (which I would not ride) and I thought he said, *No.* I settled into my seat, passed through a long, lit tunnel, and then the track went up, and the wheels started that clicking and I knew I was undone. I squeezed my eyes shut, hunched down in my seat, and started to scream.

In the year that King Uzziah died . . . Isaiah heard the sound of the wheels clicking, as he tells us of the beginning of his life as a prophet, and said, *uh oh.* In the year King Uzziah died, an age ended. Uzziah ruled in Judah for fifty-two years. During his long and peaceful reign, the world was safe. The Philistines and Ammonites were subdued. Technology flourished, nurtured by a king who appreciated creativity. Cities were built, towers fortified, cisterns dug deep into the earth to pool the sweet water for the nourishment of the wealthy and fattened herds of a satisfied and affluent people. Uzziah did what was right in the sight of the Lord, and he slept with his fathers, but after that, nothing was ever the same again. The kings who reigned were evil, no one could control their destiny nor make sense of the newly terrible way of the world, and thus golden Judah began her long, slow slide into exile. Isaiah stood at the end of a time and at a beginning: and he saw the Lord.

17. Leonard Pitts, *Miami Herald*, January 25, 1997.

In the year King Uzziah died, Isaiah had a choice, just like we all do: stay on the ground, excusing ourselves with our assertions of powerlessness and futility; or to risk everything. To screw his eyes shut, scrunch down and pray in despair, or to acknowledge that we are in way over our heads, and scream all the way down with our hands outstretched toward the future, hoping for the best. Isaiah had that choice as we do, and *in the year King Uzziah died,* when he saw the Lord *high and lifted up,* he cried, *woe is me! I am lost! For I am a man of unclean lips, and I live among a people* just like me—[18]

Now, it is customary to describe Isaiah's vision as a conversion experience, and so it was. And it is usual to say that the action of the angels and the burning coal from the altar of God took away Isaiah's sin, and it did. But what "sin," exactly, did it take away? What made him stop screaming and sit up instead and enjoy the ride?

Before we try to answer that question, I want to turn for a few moments to the work that Isaiah was called to do—the work that Isaiah was in the midst of already, when he took time to go back and remember that glowing moment that God called him to be a prophet, the voice for God in the heart of a dark and terrible time. And God said—

Go and tell the people
"Listen hard, but you aren't going to get it.[19]
"look and look—but don't understand what you're seeing"
Isaiah, tell the story and speak the word until the people tune you out
Until they tell you to get lost
Until they block their ears and cover their eyes
 Speak until your words go in one ear and out of the other—
Because they don't want things to get any better,
And nothing you say is going to help.

And Isaiah said—
It's a hard thing you're asking Lord:
To be hated by my family, to be silenced by my friends
To drive my community to distraction and despair
To watch while they cause themselves pain I can't do a thing about
And he said—*how long is it going to be like this?*
 And the Lord said—
it'll be a cold day in hell before things get any better than they are—

18. Isaiah 6:5, NRSV.
19. Isaiah 6:9, Peterson, *The Message,* 1216.
20. Isaiah 6:9-13, author's paraphrase.

cities will burn, the people will be driven away,
the countryside will be a vast and echoing wasteland
Toughen up, Isaiah, it's not getting any better in your lifetime.[20]

And, would you wonder what Isaiah's "sin" might have been? Why he might have cried out—*I can't do it, it's too hard!* Why *woe is me!* would have been the least of it?

No, Isaiah didn't commit "a" sin, nothing bad enough to keep him from God's side, anyway—it just felt that way—it felt so bad, he came *undone*. That is, with things as bad as they were, and him as small as he was, he stopped seeing the love of God and only saw his own shortcomings and frailties. What had to be done was so big, so hard that he could not see or hear anything but his fear. On the way down, he was screaming so loud he could not hear the whispering of the love of God, nor feel the hand holding his. God was still speaking, but terror rendered Isaiah blind, deaf and dumb.

So Isaiah was the perfect person for the job: because he knew exactly how it felt to be so scared, so small, and so alone that it seems like there is no way out: not now, not ever.

And that is how we feel. Our family watched Al Gore's *An Inconvenient Truth* over the Christmas holiday. And when we began to watch, we thought, *gosh, Al Gore looks tired, he looks like a wreck*. And then we listened for a while to the facts and the science and the future of a world plummeting down the roller coaster of global warming and I thought, *whew, well, no wonder! I'm tired, too. Wow, are we undone.*

That is how we feel, when we cry with Isaiah *woe is me*. For the state of the world, or for the state of our soul. The screen goes dark and the ride stops and we think: I cannot possibly get up and do this all over again.

How brave it was of the prophet to tell us the truth. To let us know how hard it is, even when God is still with us. To share the beauty of the vision with us, and the power of being healed from his fear, but not to hide the price he paid to be God's man in the world. Isaiah told the truth-and because he did, he left us a holy seed in the midst of a ruined forest; a harness to secure us and a hand to hold when the car goes plummeting down the back side of the track. He proved that it can be done—that you can ride the roller coaster and still prove that God is in the world—even and especially when everyone else is blind, deaf, and mute to the possibility that God is still speaking.

I was in a conversation the other day with a woman in our church, who said she and her partner and their seven year old daughter were struggling with a school assignment that felt so overwhelming they did not know how to start. It was a family tree, with places for the mother, the father, the grands, and so on . . .but you know, her family does not look like that: her universe is not so ordered and predictable. She has two mommies and a little sister, and came into their lives through the gift of a biological mother in China. Where to start? How to follow through? From every direction, what can be said is not enough, and may bend the tree in the wrong direction altogether, stunting its growth, its future. The whole truth does not fit neatly into the old template, but anything less, leaving it unsaid, would be a lie, a burned over stump. But this child of God and her family kept working it, and did not let frustration close their eyes or ears. And it looks this way: there is a place for her birth mother in the roots of the tree, deep in the soil of China. And there is a trunk woven out of the lives of the mothers and their families, and a branch for her sister, and healthy growing leaves for a tree that will surely be *for the healing of the nations*.[21] And the best is the last: over her tree, surrounding it and holding it up, the very air being breathed and the blue sky behind, is God. God is the one who is over the tree, says the girl, above, around, and within, the one who makes it grow.

See—Isaiah's God was saying it right, all along: *the holy seed is the stump.*[22] Amen.

SEASON OF EPIPHANY

Genesis 45:1–15   *Luke 6:27–38*

Benedictions and Beginnings

Twenty-three years is a long time. A long time to nurse a grievance. A long time to fan the flames of vengeance. I received a call from a friend in another state recently who told me that she was about to be ruined by a mistake she made twenty-three years ago. Silently, I listened while she

---

21. Revelation 22:2, NRSV.
22. Isaiah 6:13, NRSV.

poured out the painful details: what she had done; how she had tried to make amends and believed herself forgiven; how she had continued in apparently friendly relationship with the other party for years since; in what ways her work and life had changed because of that sad and terrible time. *Now*, she said, *they say there can be no forgiveness until I am made to pay. And that unless I heal the relationship there will be no justice, and no peace. And I want to heal it . . .* her voice dropped off in resignation. *But if they do not want to be healed? . . .* I ventured. *Twenty-three years is a long time*, she sighed.

We are not told how long Joseph lived in Egypt before that day came when he faced his brothers across eleven sacks of grain and a silver cup and wept. It could have been twenty-three years: doubtless, it was a long time. It was long enough for the child Joseph, sold into slavery, to grow into manhood. It was long enough for the spoiled brat who had taunted his brothers with his father's favoritism and who had lorded it over them with dreams of power to develop iron in his own soul—long enough to pass through slavery and betrayal, imprisonment and freedom, into his own power at Pharaoh's right hand. Long enough to learn that dreams, after all, belong to God. It was a long time, but it was not long enough to forgive. Not long enough for a father's grief to run its course. And not long enough for his brothers to forget what they had done to their father's favorite son and to live consumed by their guilt and their fear that, one day, they would have to pay.

It was a long time, but was it, for any of them, long enough? Was it long enough for Joseph and the ten to explain to the child Benjamin, the hostage of revenge, what was happening before his eyes that day? How long is long enough? What does it take, in our lives and in the economy of God, for a different possibility to emerge? For the suffering and the guilt, the blaming and regretting, to have gone on long enough? What does it take to let go, and to go on? Joseph's story struggles to understand—and it wants us to struggle—for understanding, for healing, for a way out of our hopeless enslavement to those things that we cannot change and that will not heal. And it wants us to believe that somehow, the power of God is at work in such endings for good, if we want it.

In the early 1980s, the United Methodist Church published an unusual liturgy—a liturgy that was received, as I remember, with scorn and indignation by the religious press and with extreme discomfort by the church-going public. It was a Ritual for the Failure of a Marriage—and its intent was to provide a place within the sanctuary of the Christian community for two partners to acknowledge their brokenness, their sorrow, and their repentance: to give thanks for what was good in the marriage that was ending, and to ask forgiveness—of God, of each other, and of the covenant community—for that which was not; and then, to let go and go on. The seminary professor who wrote the service was ridiculed in the religious press, and when the Methodist Church was accused of "encouraging" divorce, the service, with its powerful witness to the forgiving power of God, disappeared quietly into Protestant limbo.

It is possible that the uncomfortable public knew something that the church was not willing to admit . . . that our hatreds and our guilt are more preferably our own business, not God's. It may be that God has a tough time gaining a foothold on the wind blasted face of our unforgiving and unforgiven lives. For we have battered our relationships with refusals and with silence. We have smoothed out our rough edges with soothing notions of victimization and oppression, oiling them with small revenges richly deserved and deeply enjoyed. Between the roles of victim and oppressor, there is little enough room for humanity, let alone Divinity, to enter in.

All across the planet, people are squaring off against their enemies: offended, guilty, suspicious, belligerent, and afraid. We lock our doors by day and by night. We hunch behind tinted windows when need takes us through neighborhoods unlike our own. We calculate our differences as though being "other" makes one somehow less than human. And if the world is bad, the church is not much different—the church that cannot decide from one year to the next whether to tolerate or flee, whether to embrace or to run away.

In the Bible, at the beginning that is the end of Joseph's story, here in the forty-fifth chapter of the book of Genesis, Joseph stands gloating before his brothers. All the power, all the advantages are in his hands at last. He had justice on his side—and who could blame him, if he chose to revenge himself upon the brothers who had abandoned him and sold him into slavery? All the years of his life, through his story of victimization and suffering, imprisonment and finally, victory, he lived with the knowledge that "they" had done this to him . . . and now "they" were before him, helpless: and one of them was speaking—quietly, humbly, hopelessly. *What can we say? You have our lives and the life of the boy in your hand.*

For when we return to our father and he sees that the boy is not with us, then, as his life is bound up in the boy's life, when he sees that he is not with us, he will die.[23]

It is a matter of life and death. This is where we are, whenever we face the choice to forgive, have the chance to make amends, take the opportunity to face and face down our guilt and get on with our lives. In the broken and troubled family of Joseph, that time is before them as the brothers stand arguing over possession of the child Benjamin. Will his life be saved or lost? Will the family's history be redeemed, or damned? Joseph has triumphed over his own history, and stands now with the power to destroy his family's life with a word, forever. He can finish off *his* story with triumph, and doom *theirs* to never-ending sorrow.

The problem is, which story is "his" and which, "theirs?"

The question is could God make out of this end a beginning from which all twelve brothers might find a way home?

Then Joseph could no longer control himself before all those who stood by him, and he cried out: send everyone away! And he wept so loudly that the Egyptians heard it and the whole household of Pharaoh heard it. And he said to his brothers, I am Joseph! Is my father still alive?[24] When the brothers learned that it was Joseph who stood before them, they were horrified, and then afraid. And Joseph, after years of bitterness, years of grieving, years of learning and long seasons of becoming, looked at his revenge lying out before him and saw . . . the hand of God. *I am your brother Joseph whom you sold into Egypt, he said.*[25] Not Zaphenath-paneah, the powerful Egyptian potentate. Not the spoiled, blustering, arrogant favorite of Jacob, clothed in his amazing coat of many colors. Not the pitiful victim of his brothers' wrath, but only Joseph, a man who has learned to be human, and who has understood at the end of his story, that the hand of God is in all such endings, that we might begin again. *Do not be afraid! Even though you intended to do harm to me, God intended it for good: so have no fear, I will provide for you and for your little ones.*[26] Thus the broken bread of one family's sorrow became a sacrament by which the world was saved.

---

23. Genesis 44:30–31, author's paraphrase.
24. Genesis 45:1–3, NRSV.
25. Genesis 45:4, NRSV.
26. Genesis 50:20–21, NRSV.

Tuning My Heart

Only one time in twenty years of ordained ministry have I been asked to extend the church's benediction over the breaking of a marriage. Lulled by the wisdom of the world that separates light from darkness inalterably and denies the workings of God amidst the wreckages of pain and failure, it had never even occurred to me to offer. Still, in a vision born from courage and grief, the need for a greater good gave voice to the possibility of a different kind of reconciliation: *the presence of God blessed the beginning of this marriage. Let the presence of God be here, at the end.* And in the dimness and coolness of a darkened sanctuary, across a world of broken dreams, voices spoke and answered, prayers were made and blessings offered. Grace moved in the quiet there, where a few only were gathered; and at that ending, a new beginning was made, for God can turn to good whatever is broken and shared, if we will only lift up our hearts to the Lord.

SUNDAY OF THE TRANSFIGURATION

Matthew 17:1-9   *Exodus 34:29-35*

Till We Have Faces

Lent came early for me this year—this past Tuesday, at 5:30 in the afternoon, to be precise. I had stopped at Pollo Tropical, in a big hurry as usual, to buy my daughter some supper before I went to a meeting at Temple Israel. As I jumped out of the car, a man moved in front of me, his hand outstretched. *Do you have some change, lady?* I did not, and I said so, with as much kindness as I could muster. *How about a dollar, then*, he continued, pressing closer, and I noticed he had been drinking. I felt pressured, intimidated and then, unaccountably, angry. Angry and cornered. I had only four dollars and five minutes, and a child to feed. Assessing my resources, I determined that grace was in short supply. The man turned away, moving toward the next car in the lot. As he went, I realized that I couldn't remember his face. Lent came with the unbidden thought, *I am not the person I want to be.*

Lent actually begins Wednesday, and today, the final Sunday before the six-week solemn observance of that holy season, is called "The Transfiguration of the Lord." I have always liked to think of it as a kind of biblical Shrove Tuesday or Mardi Gras—a moment of joy, a surprise party of astonishment and wonder before we get down to the hard work of Lent: that long, hard season of reflection and penitence as the church looks back at the suffering and death of Jesus of Nazareth. A time to examine who we are in the reflected light of God's transforming presence . . . and having seen, to decide what we might need to do about it. Teetering recklessly on the edge of Lent, Transfiguration Sunday dares us to consider the possibility of a season of penitence marked as much by joy as by ashes, more filled with light than shadowed over by gloom and despair.

The marriage of such extremes is no easy matter, for the compromises of incarnation are difficult, and rare. The stories in Exodus and in the Gospel of Matthew describe how vast is the gulf we perceive that separates divine majesty from mere mortality, joy from despair, the knowledge of God from the human arena, *where we see through a glass, darkly*.[27]

When the Law was received by the Hebrew wanderers in their desert journey, Moses alone braved the terror of holy Sinai. It was no safe place for the people of God: as he went, the story says, the cloud covered the mountain, and the glory of the Lord settled on Mount Sinai. But in the sight of the people of Israel down below, the appearance of the glory of the Lord was like a devouring fire. And they were afraid. Later, the story tells us, when Moses came down the mountain, the marriage of glory and dust was manifest in him. Having twice braved the terror and the holiness of sacred Mount Sinai, he came back to his people a changed man, though he did not know it. *The skin of his face shone*, the story says, *because he had been talking with God*.[28] Moses received the law, he knew God face to face—he was a man so stripped of the barriers of artifice, so attuned to truth, that, though he thought he was just the same as he had always been, *his face shone*. And the people could not bear it; afraid, perhaps, that what he knew and what he had become in the presence of God was "catching," somehow: that it would erode the compromises the rest of them had made with truth in order to bear their lives as wanderers and exiles. Shining in the transfigured face of Moses was evidence that the glory of God could peacefully coexist with and in mere humanity—but the people could not bear it. So Moses veiled his face—literally covering up the evidence of God and freedom that shone so visibly from his soul—and thus

---

27. I Corinthians 13:12, KJV.
28. Exodus 34:29, NRSV.

comforted and diminished, the people could stand once again for him to live among them.

The Gospel describes how Peter and James and John went up on the mountain with Jesus, alone, and there, saw him transfigured—covered with glory and shining with light. What this passage does not tell you is that this transformation was bought by Jesus at the cost of acknowledging his impending death. Six days earlier, Matthew tells us, echoing consciously the season of Moses' incarceration on holy Sinai, Jesus, fast on the heels of Peter's astonished recognition—*You! You are the Christ, the son of the living God*—had an epiphany of his own, and came to the understanding that his ministry was to end in his violent death.[29] When the three disciples go to the mountain with Jesus, they were confused and saddened over Jesus' sudden and stubborn insistence that what little remained of his life was to be given over to suffering, betrayal, and death. When the moment of transfiguration came, that Jesus was overshadowed with all the power and the glory of God, it must have seemed to the three that what had been intimated before was merely a bad dream. Here, surely, was divine confirmation that the way of the Christ was a way of glory, not death.

It is good that we are here, Peter said, his earnest peasant face glowing with hope and the joy of their sudden release from the shadow of death, *let us build three dwellings, one for you, one for Moses, and one for Elijah, and never let this moment go.*[30] And for a moment, it was good.

This is how it must have been for Peter and the others—waking to glory, they forgot how things really were; remembering, they moved with a heart-wringing vulnerability to hang on to the dream that was already fading before their very eyes. And it did fade—so that even as Peter spoke, hardly knowing what he was saying, the glory drained away from the face of Jesus; Moses and Elijah disappeared, and a cloud overshadowed them, and they were afraid. And as the holy cloud thickened into a cold fog around the four men, Peter realized that even the blessing and the presence of God could not save Jesus from his fate. *This is my Son, my chosen*, said the voice with infinite pride and aching sadness, *listen to him*. And the story ends, *and when they heard this, they fell to the ground and were overcome by fear.*[31]

---

29. Matthew 16:16, NRSV.
30. Matthew 17:4, paraphrase.
31. Matthew 17:6, NRSV.

Hints of Dreams

Two nights after I turned away from the face of that homeless man, I had a dream. In my dream, I was traveling with my family on vacation. In the airport crowd, I was separated from them unexpectedly. I realized that I had no identification, no money, and no tickets. I could not remember what airline I was to be traveling on. I tried to persuade the airline employees that I was a legitimate traveler, a person of reasonable means, but they were unmoved: I was without resources, I had no face. I backed away, angry, and discovered that I was on a bus, riding through small, impoverished neighborhoods in a strange city. I did not know where I was, and everyone I implored regarded me with suspicion and hostility. I had been transfigured into a person whom no one knew.

I was afraid. When I woke up, I realized that I had in fact had a face: and that my face was the face of the homeless man I had refused on Tuesday afternoon.

Transfiguration is not a great escape—a way out of the troubles of the world to day-trip in glory with God, free from the terrors of responsibility in the world. Nor is the transfiguration only for the divine among us, too holy and ethereal for mere mortals to apprehend. Transfiguration is, rather, the place where two worlds meet: incarnation. All the possibilities of God embodied in the lives of people who, step by step and choice by choice, work their way up the mountain into some kind of enlightenment. It is difficult and dirty work: and it is also the glory of God, of God with us, *Emmanuel*.

Till we have faces, and see the face of the other, God cannot transfigure us.[32] And the work of transfiguration is about finding our faces and our true selves. It is about facing our hopes, and claiming them. Facing our fears, and letting them do their new and strange work in us. It is like Bill Clinton stopping short at the shouted, cynical question of a reporter—*Mr. President, will you forgive and forget?* and saying, his face shining with a strange glory: *I believe that if you need to ask for forgiveness, you must be prepared to give it*. It is the old King Hussein of Jordan, may his memory be blessed, crawling on his hands and knees in the dirt before the seven Israeli families who had lost daughters due to the insane and murderous rage of a Jordanian soldier on the Isle of Peace in the river between the two nations, begging forgiveness of his enemies. In humiliating himself, he was transfigured by glory, and became an icon of peace. It is the hard

---

32. This phrase, and the sermon title, are taken from *Till We Have Faces*, the eponymous 1956 novel by C. S. Lewis.

work each of us do every day through the confusion and the ambiguity and the difficult decisions to find out the ways and the wills of God, and to do them. It is to see the faces of glory, and to ourselves shine with it.

We sit here at the edge of Lent, on the Sunday of the Transfiguration, looking up at mountains that are both holy and distant to us. We are preparing to make a journey, too, if only a figurative one. And the question before us is this: will we have faces—and will we see the face of our neighbor? If we stay awake and watch, even in the midst of clouds and confusion, there is a hand, both human and divine, to reach down and bless us with enough of glory to see us through.

> *A young man's wife died, leaving him with a small son. After returning from the cemetery, they went to bed as soon as it was dark, because there was nothing else the father could bear to do. As he lay there in the darkness—brokenhearted, grief-stricken, numb with sorrow—the boy broke the stillness from his little bed with a disturbing question: "Daddy, where is Mommy?"*
>
> *The father tried to get the boy to go to sleep, but the questions kept coming from his confused, childish mind. After a while, the father got up and brought the boy to bed with him. But the child was still disturbed and restless, and occasionally would ask a probing, heart-rending question. Finally the boy reached out in the darkness and placed his hand on his father's face asking, "Daddy, is your face toward me?" Assured by his father's words, and by his own touch, that his father's face was indeed toward him, the boy said, "if your face is toward me, I think I can go to sleep." And in a little while, he was quiet.*[33]

And Jesus came and touched them and said, *do not be afraid.*

---

33. Moore, *When Grief Breaks Your Heart*, quoted in *And the Angels Wept: from the pulpits of Oklahoma City After the Bombing*, pp. 25–26.

4

When the Lights Go Down

The Season of Lent

It was one of those crisp, moonless August nights in Michigan's Upper Peninsula where I grew up, the kind of night that defied the name "summer." The mercury had dipped to the high forties, while the sugar maples trembled on the edge of turning from a lush summer green to a warning red. There was nothing to do but go to bed early, snuggled under blankets with the cat close by. Around midnight, something woke me. Shivering, I got up to close the window my father had left open earlier in the evening. I pushed aside the Venetian blind to find the window latch, and when I looked at my hand where it rested on the windowsill; it was glowing. Startled, I glanced out the window, and saw that above the field behind our home and past the roofs of my neighbors' houses, the northeastern sky was alight with an eerie, pulsing glow. Forgetful of the cold, I left my bedroom and stole downstairs and out into the backyard. Once there, I saw that the Northern Lights had filled not just the eastern sky, but also the entire heavens with a shimmering curtain of pink and green. Transfixed by beauty, I stood barefoot and alone in the wet grass, watching and waiting, turning round and round in delight as the heavens danced before me, shaking in the grip of a joy so spiritual and profound that it was almost pain. I cannot say how long I stood, but at last, the Lights went down and the glory faded. I noticed that my toes were turning blue with the cold, and a sharp breeze was cutting through the thin cotton of my nightgown; so I went back into the house and up to bed.

There are times—when all the conditions are right, and if we are both lucky and attentive—when our typically conventional and inglorious lives are transformed, if just for a moment, by an experience of almost unbearable loveliness and grace. Or as Luke's story of Peter, James, and John on the Mount of Transfiguration puts it *since they had stayed awake, they saw his glory.*[1] It is good to have such moments to cling to—*good that we are here*, as Peter said to the transfigured Jesus—because such moments, and the memory of them, sustain us during the hard dry seasons.

Lent is such a season: the lights go down, and we stand shivering in the dark hours of early morning, alone. The glory of the transfigured Jesus fades into clouds and doubt, and the disciples must descend from the mountain in the shrouded dark, to face weary, unfinished labors and the knowledge that the hour of Jesus' death is approaching with swift, merciless certainty. Lent is hard work: a season of reflection, prayer, and purification. A journey of solemn companionship with Jesus and the disciples, as they make their slow, sad way toward Jerusalem and the end of Jesus' life.

Most churches do not do so well with Lent. The postmodern, seeker-oriented church would not want to scare visitors away with old-fashioned notions of judgment, repentance, and self-denial. God is love, right? And love is supposed to make you feel good, and good about being in church. Anyway, most of us think we have been wounded enough by life on the outside, so that the Lenten act of deliberately entering into self-examination or, God forbid, self-critique, feels over the top, self-abusing, even.

As the humorist Garrison Keillor puts it, it is as if we have been handed a note from Mother Church, to be carried in the pockets of the faithful, reminding any who come into contact with us *Be kind to my boy. He has Been Through A Lot.* Repentance and mortification—even in its milder, spiritualized form—is archaic, primitive, obsolete, and we kinder, gentler Christians want nothing to do with it.

There is no way around it: Lent is a desert season, harsh and barren, when our serious obligations, our anxious struggling, our awareness of the fragility of our lives and the lives of those we love are permitted, even coaxed, out of the places where our deep sadness and our anxiety lies hidden in shadow to rise to the surface and be examined in the clear light of day. Facing what we are, and what we have failed to be or become, we know ourselves fragile, earthy, fallible, and we admit, even if just for a moment, that we are not all we are cracked up to be, or even quite what we have pretended.

---

1. Ezekiel 37:7, NRSV.

A friend of mine says: being made from earth is a tricky thing. On the one hand, we say *dust you are and unto dust you shall return.* And that is a hard truth. Indeed, these old words from the book of Genesis, from the heart-breaking chapter of humanity's expulsion from Eden, are the very words we use on Ash Wednesday, when the few faithful come trembling to receive the anointing of ashes and oil, the burden of their humanity. Yet on the other hand we also say: *God made humanity from the dust of the earth, and breathed into them the breath of life, and the man became a living soul.* And that is true, as well: that our earthiness, our impermanence, is our glory, our malleability, the "stuff" of which our lives are formed in the *imago Dei*, the place where the God-breath dwells, incarnate, in *our* human form.

And so this work of dust and ashes, hard though it be, must also be seen as God-work. It is God-work that frees us from the burden of illusion, pretense, and self-delusion. God-work that permits our feet, like Moses', to walk unshod on holy ground, and, having left that moment of encounter with the Flame of God that burns and is not consumed, to return, to repent, and to go another way. There is, in fact, a tradition in *kabbalah*, Jewish mysticism, which teaches that a different way to translate the Hebrew for *take off your shoes* is *change your habits.* This is necessary work for us, good work. Lent is a time for letting go, for changing bad habits, for believing that the dry work of the desert can bring us, by hidden paths, back once again to the foot of the mountain of holiness, where God still dwells in glory, awaiting us.

The Season of Lent

Genesis 2:15–17; 3:1–7

Sacred Space

Set aside, just for a few minutes, everything you think you know about this story. How God set for Adam and Eve just one restriction, one limitation. How the serpent—*more crafty than any other wild animal that the Lord God had made*—beguiled Eve, tricked her out of what she knew and seduced her with what she wanted.[2] How she longed to be wise, and took the fruit, and shared it with her husband ... and they both disobeyed God,

---

2. Genesis 3:1, NRSV.

and were cast out of paradise. Forget original sin, the apple, the snake . . . forget it all, and listen to something new.

I heard a story the other day about one of the old Jewish mystics who was called the *Baal Shem Tov*, the Master of the Good Name. He was a very holy man, and very serious about prayer. It's said he was in a certain town one Shabbat and went from place to place, looking for a synagogue in which to pray. But after stopping in at several, he turned away without entering, and went on, looking. At one synagogue, someone followed him out and said,

> *Master, why do you not enter and pray here? And he said, I cannot go in. It is crowded with teachings and prayers from wall to wall and from floor to ceiling. How could there be room for me? And when he saw that those around him were staring at him and did not know what he meant, he added: The words from the lips of those whose teaching and praying does not come from the hearts lifted to heaven, cannot rise, but fill the house from wall to wall and from floor to ceiling.*[3]

That is the story. I like this story because it is what I want prayer to be in my life: communication from heart to heart. And because sometimes, prayer is, instead, like the other thing: like words piling up. And so I have been looking for a way to make prayer new again: and I have found this brass bowl, like one that Buddhists use to sound a tone and then meditate and pray into that tone, and into the silence that follows. So, from time to time now I am using this bowl, from a tradition that is strange to me, to make prayer once again new, a holy space for connection with God.

This is what Eve and Adam had, at the first, what I am seeking with my prayer bowl: a sense of newness, of holiness, of almost unbearable sacredness—a sense of the holy so profound that when Eve felt it, she spoke with awe of the tree—*we cannot even touch it, or else we'll die.* Close your eyes . . . and remember. Remember a time you felt that way about anything: the first time you held your newborn child, your grandchild . . . the first time you loved your spouse, and the peace of being held in someone's arms . . . a sunset, a view from a certain place that was so ineffably beautiful that pain pierced through you while you watched, and you could scarcely breathe . . . a song so hauntingly lovely your eyes filled with tears as you heard it. You could hardly bear it—it touched you so deeply, it was like seeing the face of God. Remember?

---

3. Buber, "The Crowded House of Prayer," 73.

Now remember again, and again. Now go beyond remembering, and begin to worry, to contrive: *how can I have that feeling . . . that touch, that music, always? How can I make sure I see that view forever, that it becomes mine, to keep or to share as I choose?* Now: buy the CD, pop it in your car player. Play that wonderful song every day, every time you get into the car—play it over and over until at last, you cannot remember when you did not know it by heart, or comprehend why it moved you so in the first place. Remember with regret the perfection of your infant son, your tiny granddaughter—run the video over and over and over again, until the child that was seems more desirable to you than the young woman, the teenager, the adult he has become, and regret what you have lost. Become so used to loving another that your loving becomes perfunctory, routine. Buy the land where that perfect view can be seen, and build a house, and situate the window just *so*. Own the view, point it out to your friends and be proud that it belongs to you alone, become so familiar with it that in time, you do not even see it when you sit down in the chair to read the paper—because you know you can see it again tomorrow, any time you want.

Now hear the story's words about Eve and the fruit, the holy fruit from the sacred tree, and tremble as you anticipate what she and Adam are about to lose: *When the woman saw that the tree was good for food, and that it was a delight to the eyes, and that the tree was to be desired to make one wise, she took it . . .*[4]

She took it, and it became *hers, theirs*—they owned it, and it ceased being a gift. Here's the thing: we make commodities out of what is holy. We yearn for it, and experience it, and want it again, and find a way to *have* it. To give it away, to call it on demand, to sell and to buy. We take for our own possession what was a holy gift: and just like the serpent said, we become like God, owners and managers of the sacred. We take the fruit, the song, the love, the view, the relationship—we *take* it—and, in our own minds, we become godlike—able to call the sacred on demand—and when we think we are able to do that, every holy gift slips through our fingers like water through a sieve, and something in us begins to die.

I have been seeing a commercial on television recently—I think it is for some high-speed wireless Internet service. A man is surfing the net, enjoying its endless wonders and opportunities, consumed with the thrill of exploration, when suddenly, a voice from the computer speaks: *You*

---

4. Genesis 3:6, NRSV.

have reached the end of the Internet. You must go back. And his face falls, and he stumbles back from the computer into his living room, where his wife sits reading. *I thought you were surfing the net*, she says. And he replies, with a look of emptiness and loss on his face, *I finished it.*

When Eve and Adam took the fruit of the sacred tree, and made it a commodity, an everyday thing no different than any other, they finished it, and they were finished. They were finished, and they began to die. They saw they were naked, bare—stripped of their capacity to be moved, to be free, to be surprised—and, grieving and angry, they made clothes to cover their loss, and began to try to recreate, to recapture what they had lost. But all their labor gave them was a life of empty, bare, and barren hiding.

We need the holy in our lives to thrive. We need to play, or else we begin to die. We need to be surprised by love, stunned at a certain view, vulnerable to another, able to feel and experience something we have never felt or experienced before. We are made this way, to crave the surprise of the sacred, and when we try to master it, to control it, to possess it, we begin to die, understanding what we have lost. And having lost what most matters in life, what choice do we have except to cover our loss up? To cover up our pain, our lack of wonder, our loss of human-ness in defensive clothes: clothes of cynicism. Of disinterest. Of shame, or guilt. Of blame. Of feigned—or God help us, real—boredom.

This is how we live—as those who once knew what holy was, but let it go.

Recently, our family went to see the *Cirque du Soleil*, a stunning poetry of movement, story, celebration, and song. The circus—full of fantasy, surprise, beauty, and mystery—began when a little girl, sitting bored in the living room with her mannequin parents, followed a mysterious man with an umbrella out the door into an electrical storm. For more than two hours we traveled with her in this sacred place of fantasy and play, with gymnasts, tumblers, dancers, flyers, and clowns. Her awe at this world of mystery and grace was visible. Also visible, from time to time, in the midst of it all, was her father, walking with his briefcase, standing with the open newspaper, oblivious both to the delights unfolding around him and to his daughter's deep longing to share the holiness of imagination and play with her family. When sacred mystery walks in the door unexpectedly, some follow—but others hide behind the paper.

The Genesis story says that when God saw how his children were hiding, how miserable they were, how pathetic the defenses they had erected against their loss and emptiness and pain, God spoke, and God acted. God made for Adam and Eve new clothes, artfully wrought, and put them out of the Garden. For the Garden had become for them a place of loss and regret; so God was merciful, and sent them out onto a new journey to a new place. It was a place they never found, a place we have not yet wholly gotten to. On the journey to this new place, Adam and Eve recovered their love, experienced new pain, birthed children for the future, became partners with the land. And in each new thing they found, or experienced, or felt, there was a holy gift.

On our journey to this new place, we continue to do the same. We struggle with our need to have and to hold, and we seek the places where holiness is still to be found. Because we are believers, we trust that God is gifting us day by day: and that on this journey in which sometimes we have lost so much, or taken for granted more than we should have, there is still the probability, the chance, the hope that if we walk through the door, and even out into the storm, we will find ourselves in the midst of magic. This is the work of Lent, the work of relinquishing our pretense and our false hiding; the work of getting out of the ruined gardens of our lives, and setting our feet on a journey to a new place. It is a work not of our own making, but of God's, and it is to God that we ought to offer up the fig leaves that have failed to save us, holding our arms just so, as God slips a new and more suitable garment over our heads. God is doing this new thing in us, and for us. We need to try not to try so hard. We need to remember how to play. We need to risk a little nakedness, a little exposure: some surprise, some wonder, some grief, some joy. We need to stop videotaping our vacation, and start experiencing it. We need to be there—that is, to be *here*, in our own lives, where the tree of life is, where God is, and where God has been all along, gifting us wholly, with a holy new life.

SEASON OF LENT

John 2:13–25   *Exodus 20*

The Wailing Wall

In April of 1963, on the very day Martin Luther King Jr. bonded out of the Birmingham jail, a man described by historian Taylor Branch as an "obscure kook" walked up to the White House gate with a letter for President

Kennedy.[5] In the season of pain that shaped the early days of the Civil Rights Movement, serious and mammoth forces struggled for power, for justice, for privilege. William Moore, our "obscure kook," was by contrast, neither a mover nor a shaker. He was a white postman from Baltimore, and his letter informed Jack Kennedy that he was about to take ten days vacation to walk from Chattanooga, Tennessee, to Mississippi, wearing two signboards: *End Segregation in America* and *Equal Rights for All Men*. He offered to deliver any letters Kennedy might have for folks along his pathway, saying, *I intend to walk right up to the governor's mansion in Mississippi and ring his doorbell*, presenting him with a civil rights plea to *be gracious and give more than is immediately demanded of you.*[6] Though people along the way shouted threats and said he'd never make it alive, Moore said he'd grown up in Mississippi, and he knew folks weren't like that. William Moore walked for three days, but the next morning, he was found dead on US Highway 11, still wearing his signboards. Reporters later discovered that he had published a book after an earlier stay in a mental hospital, and quoted him posthumously:

> *I took my teachings literally, and where the world was not like the ideal, I believed the world was wrong and so did not adjust my behavior to reality. The dream which led me to the state hospital still has possession of me . . . my whole future is in your hands. I can only give my life, and you must make it or break it for me.*[7]

What teachings might lead a man to lay down his life for a doomed and quixotic mission?

Take these things out of here! shouted another outraged soul; an obscure teacher whom some have called a kook, *stop making my father's house a shopping mall!* And making a whip of cords with as much deliberation as William Moore must have lettered his sandwich boards, Jesus drove all of them out of the temple in Jerusalem, sealing his own doom in the process. What kind of teachings—what sort of vision—what driving passion might push a man like Jesus to risk his whole ministry at its very outset with such a violently out of character act as the cleansing of the temple?

The Synoptic Gospels, Matthew, Mark, and Luke, make it much easier for us to understand this story than does the Gospel of John. Each

---

5. Branch, *Parting the Waters: America in the King Years, 1954–1963*, 749.
6. Ibid., 748.
7. Ibid., 749.

of them places the cleansing of the temple near the very end of Jesus' life, after his triumphal entry into Jerusalem. The religious leaders of the people already hate him. The Pharisees and Sadducees have already vowed to seek his death. Tensions are high, pushed near to the breaking point by the gathering of the people for the feast of Passover, and it is not much of a stretch to imagine how Jesus might have been pushed over the edge by the futility of his circumstances. Then, too, Matthew, Mark, and Luke soften the confrontation: Jesus uses no whip on the sellers, he merely overturns the tables while interpreting his symbolic action with powerfully spellbinding teaching.

But there is nothing symbolic about what happens here in John's Gospel. There are no mitigating circumstances, no excuses, nothing at all by way of context. Fast on the heels of the lyrical sign of the changing of water to wine at the wedding in Cana, Jesus explodes into the holy temple, committing an apparently isolated act of random, sweeping violence, arising out of no other context than a burning passion in the heart of Jesus of Nazareth.

What did Jesus know, that we do not?

What did he see there that left his followers oblivious, yet filled him with terrible rage? What did he need, and what did he find?

I know a man who visited the Holy Land recently on vacation. He is a devout man, a decent man—a man who looks for a holy presence and a saving knowledge in even the most tentative of connections to his religious faith—in a story, a dream, an old movie about the passion of Christ. He went to Jerusalem on vacation, but I believe he hoped, in part, to find on that holy ground some tangible sense of evidence, some potent feeling of confirmation, that what he had learned and believed and hoped for and practiced all these long years was, in a word, real. But when he rode the bus down the *Via Dolorosa*, the way of tears that Jesus walked toward his death on the cross, it was narrow, it was dirty, it was crowded. The Garden of Gethsemane had a hotel in it, with a patio restaurant. The water from the Jordan River, where the Holy Spirit fell upon Jesus, is capped up in bottles and sold to tourists for American dollars. Confiding his sense of frustration and letdown to a Jewish man nearby, he was told: *go to the Western Wall and pray, and look at the golden city in the light of the setting sun.* So he did. He renewed his sense of wonder, of pilgrimage, of innocence, and he went to the Wailing Wall, and touching it, said a prayer. All at once next to him there stood a man—a man apparently native to the Land, and he spoke in a soft voice—*friend, what is your name? Your wife's name? Your children? Friend, I will say a prayer for you and for your family.* And in a moment, in murmured Hebrew, the deed was done. And the stranger's hand reached out to the foreigner as if to invite the touch of the real—and our pilgrim tourist reached out in return—to find, stuffed between the stranger's fingers, dollar bills: the price of prayer, the cost of holiness.

Can't you touch the bewilderment, the grief, the rage? Can't you feel the loss? The way it was supposed to be is no more—the *Shekinah*—the Glory of God—has faded and gone away—and the temple's wall, now as in the day of Jesus, was in that moment, just one more place to make a fast buck.

Now understand—as the gospel would have us understand—the terrible, timely passion of Jesus for the fragile gift of holiness, the endangered habitat of the presence of God on earth.

Jesus mourned and raged at the temple that long-ago day because he saw how much was lost between God and humankind when well-meaning, religious people took the easy way out and made of the *stuff* of religion—the temples and the churches, the rules and the regulations, the creeds and the customs, the way things had been and the way things should be—took all of that *stuff* that should have been for us nothing more than a tool to free the presence of the living God within and around us—took that *stuff* in the name of Jesus Christ, and placed upon it the name of God, and called it a day, and left God behind in the dust of the *Via Dolorosa*, the way of weeping, the way Jesus knew then he must take, to the cross.

This is why the Gospel of John tells us this story: so that we will be willing to remember how it feels to seek the holy and not find it: so that when it happens to us—as it does happen to us day by day and hour by hour—we will not turn aside in helpless grief, but will instead, like the postman William Moore and the carpenter Jesus of Nazareth, give ourselves up to the passion of holy rage, and act: wailing at the wall that separates us from the holy; putting our lives, and our words, and our bodies between the darkness and the Light, that the holy might again dwell easily among us, one day.

And is that not the least we can do? Does not life itself demand that of us?

A story in the *Miami Herald* Friday told the story of one suffering manatee—a creature so hobbled by the bindings that human beings wrongly value that its very life is being choked out of it—his organs eroded from the skin inward until the heart and holiness of that rare life is gone—the *Herald* told this story of the manatee called Phil, and described how an unlikely company of disciples—a photographer, a banker, a veterinarian, and others—canal watchers whose stories we do not know—have banded together for the past year to find and follow and save his life—the elusive, fragile life of one of the last manatees alive on this earth. This is a holy story. This is who we should be, disciples of Jesus the Christ: hunters and redeemers of the sacred.

In this brief and holy season of Lent, we remember our calling, we observe with solemn reverence the passionate, shining life of Jesus of Nazareth: and we honor how he, and others like him have died, in order that the holiness of God might survive in the world. And if we look around, even in the midst of fearful passion and grave concern: we will have the signs we need that what we serve is real. Today, we have each other, and we have the table. And though the table of the body and blood—the *real stuff* of the life of Jesus—is usually set with fine linen and exquisite silver, still, the reality of the cost—the cost of reality—is not covered up. When I was a very young pastor, overwhelmed by the responsibility of serving communion, I struggled each month to manage the heavy, ornate silver service with which First Presbyterian Church commemorated the death of Jesus. One Sunday as I poured the wine, the lid of the silver pitcher slammed shut. Wine, red as blood, spattered over the fine linen, over the broken bread, over the sleeve of my robe. The people who watched me gasped—and later I heard how that new so-called pastor had destroyed the dignity of the Eucharist with her sloppiness and disrespect.

I heard, too, how long it took to scour the linen clean of the marks of spilled wine. The sleeves of my alb still bear faded spots to remind me. And I remember: not just that, but what a friend told me, as in mortification I related the tale of how I had spoiled communion that difficult day. *Blood is spilled*, he said, shrugging. *It's what communion is all about.*

No matter how we try to beautify the act, communion is a messy business; a defending of the holy in our midst; the business of the overturned tables in the temple, thrown asunder that the fragile light of God might be found and redeemed; the business of God's reality. It is Jesus' blood, the Christ's sign, God's sacred life in us. No matter how hard we try, we can never scour our souls clean of that reality: thanks be to God. Amen.

Tuning My Heart

SEASON OF LENT

John 9:1–41

The Blind Leading

"The Laramie Project" is a documentary play, and now a film, based on the over four hundred hours of interviews taken with the people of Laramie, Wyoming, in the year following the death of gay college student Matthew Shepherd, whose savage beating at the hands of two young Laramie natives shocked the town and stunned the nation. The Tectonic Theater Company went to Wyoming shortly after Matthew's death to expose the face of evil. They expected a town full of intolerant bigots, an easy finger pointing excursion through the land of homophobia. What they found instead was a complicated story, less about the simple face of evil than it was about, really, the untidy, mixed-up, and complex web of relationships and rationales that push and pull us through the times and seasons of our lives. The story drew me in because it promised, I thought, a wrap-up to an upsetting and horrifying event in American culture—but it holds on to me precisely because it never delivered on that facile promise. This morning's gospel, the story of the man born blind—long, confusing, inconclusive—captivates for much the same reason.

Who sinned, this man or his parents, that he was born blind?[8] It was for the disciples, I suspect, a simple, even an idle question, offered in the expectation of a simple answer, one that would illuminate for those faithful learners the nature of sin and of God's judgment. A multiple-choice solution to one of life's great and perplexing problems: easily asked, easily answered.

Wouldn't that have been something? For Jesus just to have answered the question for a change—the man, or his folks, it does not really matter which one is guilty, just that someone is—so that we don't have to invest our time, our energy, or more importantly, our presuppositions and prejudices wading into this long-dead soul's complicated and messy life.

In a way, it hardly matters. The man born blind was just one of any number of stories told about the healing and teaching ministry of Jesus—just longer than most, and with a less-clear point. It wouldn't in fact make a very effective movie: its scenes shift back and forth aimlessly, the characters

---

8. John 9:2, NRSV.

lack depth and interest, the resolution of the plot is irritatingly ambiguous and thoroughly unsatisfying. Like a book too opaque in its storyline to sustain our interest, we are left with more questions than conclusions. Where did the man end up? What happened to his family and his synagogue? Why doesn't Jesus resolve anything with the religious leaders, or even with his disciples? Frustrated, we toss the book onto the back of the nightstand, resolving to try again at another time, perhaps when we are less tired or stressed out. But will we? Can a work so muddy and so difficult really hold our attention? Call us into intentional contemplation?

After nearly twenty years in parish ministry, the fact that nobody wants to "do Lent" bemuses me more than it upsets me. I think I have tried just about everything to invite the people of God into what the church sees as an important season of intentional contemplation. Lenten suppers, book studies. Prayer services, spiritual storytelling. Films, sermonic "homework," a shared study series with neighboring congregations, community Ash Wednesday service—just about anything anyone suggests, I'll try . . . and the same three to seven people show up. I'm not complaining—merely noting: Lent is a hard sell under any circumstances because it asks us to journey for a long time in a spiritual wilderness of hard questions and dry places. And really, that is hard enough to do when we have to, let alone that we should choose it as a recreational—I mean, a re-creational—activity on our one night off; or as a spiritual discipline laid on a spirit already weighed down with minutiae and troubles enough.

The story of the man born blind, the problem with Lent, and the documentary Laramie Project all remind me that we are mostly people who are, for what seem to us very good reasons, disinclined to immerse ourselves in complicated, insoluble questions. We would rather plan a weekend out of town than commit to a six-week spiritual journey without clear, quantifiable objectives. We appreciate the simple story, the easy answer, the thirty-second sound bite. We have little patience—or more truthfully, little spiritual energy—to spare on matters that do not mostly speak for themselves.

So—when the man born blind confronts his religious community's leaders with the messy problem of a miracle working renegade rabbi—they do not have the energy to examine the issue of how God might be at work in the life of a man they branded a Sabbath-breaking sinner—and the problem gets solved by throwing the healed man out of the synagogue. And when the man's parents are confronted by the community, they lack the energy to stand with their son and risk their place and their reputation on a question with no easy answers... so they turn their backs on their child and save themselves. He is of age, ask him. We don't know. We can't say. We don't want to get into it. Let someone else deal with it.

More than one of the families interviewed in Laramie, Wyoming, answered the question *how do you think Matthew's killing could have happened here?* with some version of *I don't know about that. What I do know is, we're all just live and let live people here. That's just our way.*

Or using the words of the great American writer O'Henry in his story, "The Unicorn in the Garden": *Shut up, she explained.*

The story in the Gospel of John invites us to consider how it might have been different for the man born blind, his family, and his community of faith if, instead of resolving the hard questions and the messy theology with the Bible version of *shut up, she explained*, they had just gotten down into the mud with Jesus, made a healing paste of the dust and the dirt and the messiness of life, and followed without anxiety or expectation wherever that unfolding possibility of a miracle of grace led them. How it might be different for us if, instead of trying to see it all and know it all, we let the blind lead the blind, and waded into the work of our complicated lives together, with hope and with patience.

When the disciples asked *who sinned, this man or his parents, that he was born blind?* they got more than they bargained for with Jesus' answer—though I think they, and we—still miss the point entirely.

Neither sinned, said Jesus, *it happened so that the work of God might be revealed.*[9] No one sinned. When these things happen—to a man born blind, to a young man born gay, to a mother, a child, a family, a father, a filmmaker, a businesswoman, a person—when these things happen to us and to others, there is no easy answer, but there is a simple solution: do not get away, but get down in the mud with whomever in your world is brave enough and messy enough to join you; and make a healing paste of the dry dust and the dirt of your life... apply it to your own eyes, and try to see the world a little differently. No one sinned—but how can we let the work of God be revealed? Where is God, or where can God be, through you, in the life of a crying child, an angry town, a disgruntled worker, a hopeless situation, an answerless question? What can you make in the mud that is beautiful, healing, transforming, or even merely useful?

---

9. John 9:3, NRSV.

Lent is about being in our lives—and in our lives' questions—for the long haul. For the interminable story, the twisting plot, the lack of clean resolution, and the sudden, blinding experience of grace that somehow points us in a new and unforeseen direction without ever, quite, wrapping up our loose ends. Maybe, when we see Lent as a chore, we miss an important opportunity. For it may be that Lent gives us permission to freely explore those questions that otherwise keep us awake at night, cut us off from friends and lovers, sap our strength until God is the adversary rather than our refuge and strength, a very present help in time of trouble.

One of the men interviewed in Laramie was an emergency room doctor who treated both Matthew Shepherd and, at the same time, one of his killers, wounded in a barroom brawl. On tape, he puzzled over his own feelings about homosexuality—*I don't approve*—and the paradox of his empathy for the suffering of Matthew and of his killer Aaron, while he labored trying to heal the dusty mess of their battered bodies. He confessed that he wasn't sleeping nights, worrying about it all, trying to figure it out, trying to forget and move on. A year later, he was interviewed again, and this is what he said: *I said before that I didn't approve, that I didn't understand . . . but it's been a year, and we've all seen such pain and waste, and for what? So I decided, there was one thing I could do, I could give it up, and just embrace . . . just embrace it all. And I don't know whether this decision is wrong or right . . . but I do know that I can sleep at night.* Maybe, like the doctor in Laramie, we would sleep better at night embracing rather than trying to shut out, wall off, close down the hard issues and the complicated stories of our lives. Maybe, if we cannot clear a night to observe Lent in the old church way of fasting and praying, we could observe Lent by getting into our lives—all of the dusty and dry stuff—not looking for quick answers, but expecting only this: that in the mud and the mess, if we are willing to get down into it, God's work will be made visible, because we at last are willing to open our eyes.

Tuning My Heart

LAETARE SUNDAY (4TH SUNDAY OF LENT)[10]

Joshua 4:19—5:12

Baggage

This day I have rolled away the reproach of Egypt.
Joshua 5:9

Here is a strange thing. When we finally are freed to leave the wilderness—when at last it is time for the, or at least, "a" promised land in our lives, and we had thought the time for choosing was past—the difficult decisions, the hard choices between lesser evils—*then* is the moment we are called to make the truly dangerous passages of our lives: to choose from the wilderness what we will leave behind, and what will become a permanent part of us, the light of the holy, carried like an ark of God into a new beginning.

This text from the book of Joshua illustrates this—*pointedly*—by observing that Joshua's little band of Hebrews, set to cross the Jordan and enter the land of promise, had at some time during their wilderness wandering ceased to observe their ritual of faith, and were uncircumcised. Those who had left Egypt bore that sign of the covenant. Those who had been born in the wilderness, had not. Poised to enter the Promised Land, the community noticed they had left the wrong things behind in

---

10. In the history of the church, the fourth Sunday in Lent (like the third Sunday in Advent, Gaudete Sunday) is a day appointed for the "lightening" of the solemnity of the Lenten season. To that end, the color of the hangings on pulpit and lectern is "lightened" from a deep, somber purple to a more hopeful rose color. The name Laetare (in Latin, "rejoice") is from the text of Isaiah 66:10–13 (NRSV) that opens the Roman Catholic Mass on that Sunday.

> Rejoice with Jerusalem, and be glad for her, all you who love her;
> rejoice with her in joy, all you who mourn over her—
> that you may nurse and be satisfied from her consoling breast;
> that you may drink deeply with delight from her glorious bosom.
> For thus says the Lord:
> I will extend prosperity to her like a river,
> And the wealth of the nations like an overflowing stream;
> And you shall nurse and be carried on her arm,
> And dandled on her knees.
> As a mother comforts her child, so I will comfort you;
> You shall be comforted in Jerusalem.

the wilderness. They had forgotten who they were, children of Abraham and Sarah, set apart, a peculiar people. *Make flint knives*, said the Lord to Joshua, and I don't need to say more, even though the Bible itself saw fit to underscore the magnitude of this re-entry into covenant community by observing that the place where all this happened was known as *Gibeath-haaraloth*, that is, "the hill of the foreskins."[11] Well, enough said.

It is human nature to want to leave the past—especially a past of wilderness wandering—behind. Entering a new marriage, who wants to remember the failures of the past? Recovering from a life-threatening illness, or the psychological damage of a childhood of abuse or neglect, who wants to be known, always and forever, as a "survivor?" George Bush does not want to make much of his own past as an alcohol abuser—he would rather, as he says, look ahead. *I used to have a problem*, we might say dismissively about whatever it was, or is—*but not any more*. It takes a rare kind of courage to continue to affirm *I am an alcoholic. I am divorced. I have a mental illness*—when to all observers, we have set things right, survived, and thrived, having put the wilderness and its baggage behind us.

In his novel, *The Inextinguishable Symphony*, Martin Goldsmith, a senior commentator for National Public Radio, tells the story of his parents' life as Jewish musicians in Nazi Germany and their miraculous escape into a new life in the United States. With the exception of his mother and father, their entire families were exterminated in the camps, victims of the Holocaust.

Goldsmith describes his family's Holocaust history as *the enormous tree growing up through the roof in the center of their family home*.[12] It was a tree that no one acknowledged, yet that cast over their lives a huge and subduing shadow. His father, he said, spoke of himself as a "so-called Jew," and it was with enormous shock that Martin discovered, in the course of researching his book, documents detailing his father's bar mitzvah in the records of the Oldenburg synagogue.

> *So how Jewish was he, really? And for that matter, how Jewish was I? I tried to learn more . . . but he steadfastly insisted that he remembered nothing about it, not even that it took place. In the same conversation I asked him if he thought of himself as a Jew. "No." he replied instantly. "But you were bar mitzvahed," I said. "You played in an all-Jewish orchestra." "Adolph Hitler thought I was Jewish, so*

---

11. Joshua 5:2–3, NRSV.
12. Goldsmith, *The Inextinguishable Symphony*, 1.

I had no choice." On we went . . . he could not bring himself to say, "I am a Jew."

Musing over the cost of that reality and its forgetfulness, Goldsmith concludes—*maybe my father says that he is not a Jew because the association is too painful. My father got into the habit of spurning that part of his identity while it threatened him . . . and once in America he found it easy to maintain the habit. Why should he be a Jew when to be a Jew brings so much pain?*[13]

Why, indeed? Why be a Jew, a Christian, a survivor, a racist, a homophobe, a failure, a divorcee, an anything that reminds us of past pain we would rather forget? What is the point of carrying the baggage of a history we have triumphantly overcome? Would it not be better, more useful, more faithful, even, to call ourselves a *new creation*, and put the past in some dark and forgotten place, never to be considered or retrieved?

The story from the book of Joshua tells us that when the massive task of community-wide circumcision was done, when the people had rested and were whole again, God spoke to Joshua and declared with satisfaction, *today I have rolled away from you the disgrace of Egypt.*[14] Now what does that mean? Is it that, having endured the wilderness and having entered the Promised Land, the shame of being known as "slaves," as "wandering Jews," as "strangers in a strange land" is finally erased? Now, we have a new job—so the shame of being unemployed is forgotten. Now, we have a new spouse—so the loneliness and stigma of being divorced is in the past. Now, we have a nice house and a healthy bank account—so the shame of being brought up poor as dirt is behind us. Is that what Andy Williams, the shooter from Santee, believed? That if he could prove his manhood with a gun in a school where he was despised and mocked, the shame of being a freak could be expunged from his soul? Do we roll away the reproach of our wildernesses, the baggage of Egypt, by overpowering and overwriting the past, or is there another, a better way? Is it true that *those who cannot remember the past are condemned to repeat it?*[15]

We dare not roll away the reproach of the past by denying and forgetting it. That is a dangerous path, indeed, upon which to set our feet. Yet it is so easy—so very easy to do—a little editing here, a small story forgotten there, a detail not mentioned. Note, for example, the disturbing

---

13. Ibid., 330-31
14. Joshua 5:9, NRSV.
15 Attributed to George Santayana, 1863-1952.

omission in this Bible story—a story that insists on remembrance, that speaks over and over again of the danger of neglecting past experience and the importance of telling the story.

It is the Passover story of which we are speaking here. And the text tells us *they ate the produce of the land; the manna ceased on the day they ate the produce of the land; they ate the crops of the land of Canaan that year.*[16] What it does *not* tell us is who tilled, who planted, who nurtured these crops from which the newly triumphant invaders of Canaan feasted? And who were they, if not those very tribes whom the Hebrews, themselves oppressed slaves, had hounded and harried out of the Land of Milk and Honey? *We were slaves in Egypt*—but now, by golly, we're going to get ours, and no one best get in our way. Did God ever mean that we should roll away the reproach of our past with acts of retaliation? Or is there a more excellent way?

There are other ways to get into the Promised Land from the harsh past of the desert—ways embodied in the biblical witness that encouraged the inclusion of strangers and aliens—*for* we *were strangers in Egypt*; ways that mine the same faith history, claim our personal stories, and acknowledge our national heritage for a history that instructs, that warns, that guides us into a new life—a new life shaped by the painful experience of the past, not distorted around it.

After the shooting in Santee, Leonard Pitts wrote a commentary in the *Miami Herald* asking, in effect, what is happening to our white children of privilege? He reminded us of how, when black-on-black violence mars the poorer neighborhoods of our communities, civic leaders are quick to make connections, recall the past, raise the wilderness issues that address what is happening to a lost generation of black boys. Remembering Santee, he notes that no one is recalling or acknowledging that the vast majority of the school shootings in the past five years in this country have been the acts of affluent young white boys—he asks, why is no one remembering? Why is no one asking *what is happening in our suburbs?* If we cannot make the connections, remember the history, face what we have been and are, *talk about it*—how can we hope to save our children for the covenant, for the future, whatever color they may be?

Remember how we began this season's Lenten journey acknowledging the wilderness? We all have them, we said, we all have wildernesses,

---

16. Joshua 5:11–12, NRSV.

and they all have three things in common: we do not choose them, we cannot control them, and however noisy that wilderness may be, the one thing not heard is the voice of God. Now, we are poised on the banks of the Jordan River, poised to enter a promised land, ready to embrace resurrection power in the Easter to come. It is Laetare Sunday—that day in the long Lenten fast for lightening up and knowing that all wildernesses have borders we must reach at last. Here, at water's edge, with the past behind us and the future unfolding before us: know this. Know that you cannot choose your wilderness, but you can choose what to do with it, and what you carry out of it. You cannot control it: but you can control yourself. And if the voice of God is silent—perhaps it is only because you have not yet told your story, or found the courage to speak.

May the words of our mouths, and the meditations of our hearts, be acceptable in your sight, or Lord, our rock and our redeemer. Amen.

SEASON OF LENT

John 12:1–8

Overdone

Boogieman George starts putting up his Christmas lights in the middle of October every year: he knows that while some things are for everyday, we do not always have Christmas. To tell you the truth, George's Christmas display could be a textbook illustration of the word tacky: every inch of the yard, front and sides, is covered with lights, stuffed animals, trains, strips of cotton "snow," plastic Santa Clauses and manger scenes crammed together helter-skelter so that you can scarcely tell where the elves leave off and the shepherds begin. It is overdone, lavish, tasteless, extravagant, brash. I love it.

But not everyone does. This past December, the *Miami Herald* carried an article about how Boogieman George was annoying our tasteful South Dade neighborhood. The music is too loud, the lights too garish, the scene not in keeping with a true sense of Christmas, they said. The article described how neighbors have erected barriers to keep George's Christmas display at bay, chronicling how a couple of his near neighbors have even sold out their homes in order to get away from what they perceive to be a gross and overbearing public display ... but more on that, later.

When the Lights Go Down

A similar phenomenon occurs when we examine the scene that opens the twelfth chapter of the Gospel of John. The disciples and Jesus are gathered in the home of Mary, Martha, and Lazarus for a pre-Passover celebration. It is an apparently quiet and joyful scene, rendered deeply meaningful by the fact that it should have been a funeral, but instead is a feast. In the previous chapter of John's Gospel, we are told how Jesus came to the home of his friends only days earlier to find Lazarus dead, and the sisters wild with grief and anger. Weeping with them, he had performed the greatest of his miracle signs in this Gospel, raising Lazarus from the dead. Now, a brother had been restored to his family, and where there was sorrow, there is joy. Jesus has returned to that place of renewed life, and the gathered family is celebrating in a scene that looks to be peaceful, orderly, civilized.

But in a moment, everything changes, though we do not know precisely how. Mary looks at the man, perhaps, while she is serving a dish, and sees somehow that the master's eyes reflect not so much the quiet and homey joy of that simple evening as something else . . . something like an almost unbearable pain. There's more to this picture than meets the eye, and she knows it. Outside that quiet house in Bethany, the story tells us, the world's reaction to Jesus' act of extravagant life-giving has been anything but joy. Rumors abound, and most of what is being said is hostile. The leaders of the Jerusalem community are out to kill Jesus and Lazarus both, and throughout the countryside, folk of all kinds are wondering and waiting and watching: when will Jesus be taken, and how? In Jesus' eyes, Mary sees that knowledge of impending doom, and the sadness it brings him, and she knows: he is going to die, and he is afraid. Even in the safe and loving embrace of the family, he is utterly alone.

In that moment, everything changes. Seized by an almost unbearable tenderness and passion, she runs for the corner of the room and snatches up the most valuable possession she has: a jar of rare, costly perfume. It is her life's savings, an investment worth perhaps ten thousand dollars by today's standards, and it is the only thing of value that is entirely her own to give, but no matter. Pushing through the gathered mass of men and cushions, food and wine, she kneels and shatters her precious bottle of ointment over the feet of the startled Jesus. As the heavy, sweet, overpowering scent of nard floods the room, the convivial conversation stops, and all eyes, shocked, turn to the woman on the floor. The perfume puddles at his feet as slowly, deliberately, she reaches both arms up over her head—

till that moment, modestly and appropriately covered—loosens the knot at the back of her head, and as the heavy dark mass of it falls around her shoulders and back, bends down to the floor, and wipes the excess oil from his feet with the shining curtain of her hair. It is a shockingly sensual moment, and now, emotions bared, the dinner party is no longer civil, and everything is out of control: as out of control as, only days later, Jesus' own life will be, as he returns to Jerusalem and spirals down to his death.

It is a moment of earth-shattering symbolic power, creating an almost unbearable intimacy—fear and love and sorrow are all there now, at table together with the friends, and nothing is hidden.

Speaking into the silence, a cultured voice profanes the intimacy hanging in the perfumed air. *Why*, the voice drawls, *was this perfume not sold for three hundred denarii and the proceeds given to the poor?*[17]

Why indeed? The moment of intimacy dissolves in the civilized common sense of Judas' inquiry, and everyone in the room breathes a sigh of relief—a sigh, alas, still heavily tainted with the remnants of the woman's embarrassing act of excess. It is astonishing how quickly even the community of Jesus will move to cover over the wild, untamed extravagances of the free spirit of love. Now in the room there is anger, self-righteousness, fear. Love is too close, and so is death. Sorrow is too much with us, and right beside it, the haunting anxiety that life has not and will not progress tidily down the narrow pathways we have established and permitted, in our carefully constructed lives. Lazarus will die, and then, unexpectedly, he will be alive again. Jesus will die, and we will be left alone. Love will overtake us, and chaos may be just around the corner. What else is there to do but take refuge in common sense?

Common sense makes us shun our enemies, and bids our friends to do the same. Love says, like Nelson Mandela did when he assumed the presidency of South Africa, *without these enemies of ours we will never bring about a peaceful transformation . . . let's sit down together and talk peace.*

Common sense keeps emotions politely hidden, changes the subject, draws attention elsewhere—love finds what is flowing beneath the surface, and sets it free.

Common sense says *waste not, want not . . .* love cannot find enough ways to express itself, and counts nothing wasted that is given for love. How often does love win out over practicality in our lives? How often do

---

17. John 12:5, NRSV.

we set duty aside to give what we have for love? Go out to play rather than do our homework? Acknowledge or ask about a deep emotion on the face of another rather than turning politely aside while they get themselves back under control? Do something entirely frivolous, merely for the sake of love?

We have no idea how potent our actions may be in the life of someone else, when we lay aside the dictates of common sense for the reckless demands of love. Adoration and excess for its own sake may seem like a frivolous exercise . . . but for the person who receives it, it may make all the difference in the world.

When Mary moved away from the feet of Jesus and raised her eyes to meet his, the haunted fear was gone from his face, and they both smiled through tears as he said: *Leave her alone. She bought it so she might keep it for the day of my burial. You always have the poor with you, but you do not always have me.*[18] And with that, he was ready. Having received out of the wasteful extravagance of the love of a woman the one gift that was needful—the chance to face and embrace the reality of his coming death—Jesus received Mary's anointing, and was at peace. And when he left the house in Bethany to face the angry mob, he was ready, and he was no longer alone.

How often do we pass up a chance to save someone's life, or heal someone's soul, by heeding the voice of common sense over the voice of love?

Well. Back on 54th Avenue in South Miami, just a few blocks from the church, the forces of common sense rallied last fall, and tried to prevail over the tacky excesses of love. The city of South Miami made Boogieman George's street one way for the duration of the Christmas display. The neighbors put up their fences and their concrete barriers and posted their "keep off this property" and "no parking at any time" signs. The city forced George to shut down his display from 10:30 p.m. on through the quiet, staid night. But Christmas, like resurrection, like love, is uncontrollable. And by the end of October, George was out building in his yard again: light by light, stuffed animal by stuffed animal, inch by inch of tacky cotton "snow" surrounding manger scenes and Santas alike: a monument to excess, a witness to a joy that will not be held down, a gaudy and eloquent testimony to love: the kind of love that sent that manger's beautiful, helpless baby boy down a lonely road that ended in his death. A death that, by

---

18. John 12:7–8, NRSV.

the way, was also a terrible, wasteful, extravagant monument to the power of God, to the love of God. Every year, I look at that old tacky manger scene, and I watch the face of that painted plastic baby, shining in the lights. And when I do, I seem to smell, if just for a moment, an almost unbearably overpowering scent of a spilled jar of expensive perfume. Oil shines on the feet of the baby, and Mary hovers nearby. And in the lights, the children's eyes, like Christ's, are shining. Amen.

SEASON OF LENT

John 11:1–44   *Ezekiel 37:1–14*

Saturday's God

Every day is a god, each day is a god, and holiness holds forth in time.[19]

It could be a nice thought, even a pleasant one. Every day is a god, and holiness is revealed as we make our way gently and peaceably through the world. A butterfly, a sunset, a cup of coffee with a friend, the cry of a newborn child, a bird on the wing. If we pay attention to the right things, every day could be a god we might be willing to worship. Kind of like a church I heard about the other day—the minister had done his doctoral work at the Crystal Cathedral in Southern California; and returning from that temple to possibility thinking, he would ask his congregation each Sunday morning, How Are You? And they would respond in a mighty chorus, *We are in a space of blessing and grace!*

Every day is a god, each day is a god, and holiness holds forth in time.[20] These are the words of the writer Annie Dillard who was not looking merely for blessing, but to understand the ways God is in the world with us. In 1975, she moved alone into a one-room cabin on a small island in the Puget Sound to ask questions about time, reality, death, sacrifice, and the will of God.

I came here to study hard things, she said, *and to temper my spirit on their edges.*[21] And she did. The burning of a moth in a candle flame, the

---

19. Dillard, *The Annie Dillard Reader*, 432.
20. Ibid.
21. Ibid., 430.

silence of God, a little girl whose face was burned by flaming jet fuel when a small plane crashed in the forest near her family's home; the minister of a tiny island church who once, *in the middle of a long pastoral prayer of intercession for the whole world—for the gift of wisdom for its leaders, for hope and mercy to the grieving and the pained, succor to the oppressed, and God's grace to all—in the middle of this he stopped and burst out, "Lord, we bring you these same petitions every week!" and then continued reading the prayer.*[22] *Every day is a god*, she said, but every day is not Sunday, and the god we may meet is not always in a space of grace and peace. *"Teach my thy ways, O Lord," is, like all prayers, a rash one*, says Dillard, *and one I cannot but recommend.*[23]

It seems to me that, if we are to be a whole people of God, a *real* people, that we must expect more from God—and from ourselves—than to feel good and happy and peaceful on Sunday morning. To be God's *real* people, is, in a way, to be like the old plush horse in the children's story, *The Velveteen Rabbit*, to know that "real" is to have one eye missing and all your fur rubbed off, because you were loving and loved, and loving means, sometimes, hurting.

To pray *teach me thy ways, O Lord*, and to mean it is to be more than Sunday Christians, to worship more than Sunday's god. Let me say what I mean. In two weeks, it will be Easter. Next Sunday is Palm Sunday, and following that, Holy Week, a time that is difficult for us to observe liturgically. Thursday—the day of betrayal, betrayal by a friend and abandonment by family. Friday—Arrest, trial, mockery, torture, condemnation, and finally, death. These days are hard for us to bear . . . and harder still, the day that comes after, the empty hours of Saturday: when the worst has happened, and we are drained and despairing, and we do not know how to hope for a Sunday resurrection. Thursday and Friday are terrible days; but Saturday, the in-between day of hopeless resignation and painful realization that what we had is gone and what will be, we don't know. The Apostles' Creed we recite, *I believe in God . . .* , presumes a Sunday faith and a Sunday god: a goal, a promise, a future: but before we can wake up on Sunday, we have to come to worship the god of Saturday.

What does it mean to know Saturday's god?

---

22. Ibid., 446.
23. Ibid., 430.

Saturday is living with the crushed hopes and the betrayal of Mary and Martha—*if you had been here, my brother would not have died.*[24] They had trusted their friend Jesus to come, but he had not, and Lazarus was dead. Saturday is juggling what we thought we believed about the reliability of our friends, of life in general, of God, against what we know and see as life's heartbreaking evidence to the contrary: *I know he will rise at the resurrection in the last day . . . I know that you are the Christ of God—but what good is that? You were not here. He is dead now, and where is God?*

Saturday is looking our losses straight in the eye: *already there is a stench, because he has been dead four days.*[25]

Saturday is being told—*the chemo isn't working, and we don't have anything left to try.*

Saturday is . . . a miscarriage, the unexpected end of a career to which you had given your youth and your life's blood, a hurricane destroying your home, being told by your spouse: *I don't love you anymore. I want a divorce.* Saturday is a lump in your breast, a tremor in your hand, a phone call at 3:00 in the morning.

Saturday is Ezekiel, in the midst of that terrible valley of dried up bones when the voice of God prodded him and goaded him and said, *mortal, can these bones live?* and the prophet sighed and said, *God knows. God knows, but I don't. Our bones are dried up, our hope is lost, and we are cut off completely. Can these bones live?*[26] God knows. We haven't a clue.

We do not know, and what is more, we do not want to admit it. And we do not want to admit, either, that we would rather not spend too much time around people whose lives are in the province of Saturday's god. It threatens us, and makes us uncomfortable, and so we say: *just believe, and everything will be fine.* We say: *this must be God's will,* when how could it be? How *could* it be? We come to church and say, *We are in a space of blessing and grace,* but it is a lie, we are not anywhere near that space, and our eyes show the truth our lips cannot bear to speak. We cannot bear Saturday, and we do not want our faith to be about Saturday's god. Sometimes we come to church to reinforce our hope that it is possible to jump from Friday to Sunday, without dealing with the pain and confusion and frustration of Saturday.

---

24. John 11:32, NRSV.
25. John 11:39, NRSV.
26. Ezekiel 37:3, 11, NRSV.

But, I know there are Saturday people among us today, and some for whom the reality of Saturday is so great they are not here today, or any Sundays. There are people here who will say when asked, *Oh, I'm fine, everything's fine*, when both you and they know it is a lie, because they do not know how to live with Saturday's god.

And there are people not here this morning, for whom the effort of getting dressed up and coming to church to say the words and go through the motions of Sunday is too much to be borne. Saturday people, who don't know that the life of faith is at least as much about what we do *before* the bones stand up and start rattling around as it is, how we celebrate *after*.

For we have to live in Saturday, before we can wake up on Sunday morning. There is just no way around it. Martha could not jump to the resurrection of her brother; she first had to deal with Saturday. Jesus hadn't come when she needed him. Her brother had died. She had to juggle the creed, what she had been taught to say, what she had been told to believe, against the sad weight of her present experience: *I know he will rise again, at the resurrection, on the last day. Yes, Lord, I know that you are the Christ of God. Yadda, yadda, I know all of the above, but Lazarus is still dead and that's what's real.* She had to go to the tomb, and remind everyone that dead things stink, and grieve what she had lost; and only then was she ready to take the next step, the step that would lead her to Sunday, and resurrection.

It was the same for Ezekiel. Living in exile in Babylon, far away from the homeland that was his heart's hope, he waited, while the reports came straggling in, frozen words of hopelessness out of refugees who looked like they had seen the pits of hell. The temple was defiled. It was burned to its foundations. Golden Jerusalem was rubble. The people were scattered. God had vanished. There was no hope. In the grip of vision, Ezekiel faced Saturday: walked around that God-forsaken place, stumbled through the scattered refuse of a disaster so sudden and overwhelming that the dead were not even decently buried. The valley was full of bones, like the pit of the World Trade Center, like the streets of Ramallah and Bethlehem and Jerusalem, like the caves of Afghanistan, like the fields and lakes behind a small crematorium in Georgia, or the desecrated Menorah Gardens right here in Miami. The world is full of bones. And Ezekiel acknowledged what we already know: they were very dry. He admitted his doubt that life could ever come again to that place. He listened to the challenge of God, and felt utterly ridiculous looking forward in hope, and he resisted until he could resist no more. And then, with a furtive glance about to see whether anyone was watching, he undertook to do the impossible, he took the next step, which led toward Sunday. *So I prophesied as I had been commanded.*[27]

It is hard to live with Saturday's god, when Sunday is where we want to be. It is hard, but not impossible. Yesterday, I went to the wedding of my young friend Alan and his sweetheart Angel. The very young minister read from the book of Genesis, looked Alan and Angel straight in the eye and said, *marriage isn't hard, you only have to do one thing. Just listen. Listen.* And I thought, wow. *Could I be brave enough to tell a young couple that? Is that enough?* Just listen.

Living with Saturday's god is like that, I think. Just listening, and praying, *teach me thy ways, O Lord.* It is a matter of taking the next step, knowing that, if the god of blessing and grace isn't with you, the god of Saturday surely is. It is doing your homework, every day, to the best of your ability. It is writing résumés, and looking through the paper, and making phone calls. It's going to therapy, or saying goodbye, or walking away from the cemetery. It is doing what you know you have to do, to get through the next minute, or hour, or Saturday.

I think the miracle of resurrection does not happen in the darkness of Sunday morning: I believe it happens in the full light of day, all day Saturday, while the long hours are passing, seemingly without hope. I think the resurrection happened when Martha stepped back from blocking her brother's tomb and let the stone be rolled away, even when she was worried about the stench and wrenched with grief and anger and embarrassment that Jesus was creating a scene at her brother's funeral.

I think resurrection happened when Ezekiel stopped worrying for a moment about the desperate and dubious dryness of that lost valley, or about how stupid he would look prophesying to a graveyard, and did what he had to do, and realized that he *could* do it. *I prophesied as I had been commanded*, he said, and there was a world of wonder and possibility in it, even before the bones rattled themselves back to life before his astonished eyes. I think resurrection begins not on Sunday morning, but on Saturday, when we take a chance and do what we know we have to do, not knowing whether Sunday will ever come.

Because we have to live in the moment, before the dead things around us and in us can begin to come back to life. It's not our job to make Sunday

---

27. Ezekiel 37:7, NRSV.

happen: we only have to stop sighing and denying and get on with it, and start walking with Saturday's god, one step at a time.

Maybe this is an abrupt place to stop a sermon, pausing in the middle of the weekend when the stories all end with resurrection joy. For after all, you could point out, Ezekiel's valley of dry bones became a village of living hope. Lazarus came out of his tomb, bound with the evidence of death but ready to live again. Resurrection is real, it happens: our faith proclaims it, our experience confirms it—sometimes, eventually. But today, two weeks before Easter, I want to honor the Saturdays of our lives. I want to take seriously the wrenching experiences of our losses, the good, hard work I have seen each of you do through the years when faced with Saturday circumstances. I want to honor Saturday's god, be open to the questions and the possibilities and the problems, so that when Sunday's spirit comes at last, we will know what it means to pray: *teach me thy ways, O Lord*, and mean every last word of it. Amen.

Tuning My Heart

HOLY WEEK TRIPTYCH

Good Friday, the Temple

bearing aloft the cries of the dying,
the hot wind sweeps
through the city
stirs
the holy place (now no longer holy,
nor defiled, for now no more alone)
lifts
the ragged edge of royal purple—
the curtain torn.

Saturday, the Upper Room

fear seals the shutters here
where no wind enters
guilt stills the air
and the voices of sorrow-suffocated souls
locked inside
are silent
they stay
upstairs

Sunday, the Garden Tomb

Whisper-cool cave air
greets the day
morning breeze mingles
outside the useless stone door
enters in,
sifts through,
sings forth:
Christ is risen.

5

The Acts of Orchids

Easter Day to Ascension

EASTERTIDE

During Holy Week a few years ago, a man in our congregation who grows orchids as a hobby brought me a gift. I can never remember its official classification, so John said I could call it an "Easter orchid." The Easter orchid was a beautiful, delicate, glorious thing, an explosion of tiny golden flowers, cascading like streams of glowing stars over the side of the plain dark wooden cage that contained its roots. It looked like molten sunlight, resurrection life spilling out of a cool dark casket. The orchid was breathtaking.

My friend John explained how I should care for this magnificent flower. He said, *you need to water it all year, until October, then leave it alone. After a few months, you'll see these little dry pods and tendrils beginning to come up from the root. They don't look like much, but that's where the flowers will be. Water them some, and then, after a while, the whole thing will be covered with those pods and tendrils . . . and then, suddenly it will bloom, just like* that, *and look like what you see here today.*

Carefully, I took the orchid home and hung it on a tree by my kitchen window, imagining how wonderful it would be to see that blooming mass of gold all summer long. But then, John's wife Vivian told me how much she loved the flowers on this kind of orchid, except for the fact that it only blooms once a year.

Once a year? I said. *That's all,* she said, smiling. For a moment, I felt utterly deflated. All that waiting and watering and watching for only *one* brief season of glory? And such a short season, too, I grieved, as the blossoms, too soon, browned and fell from the Easter orchid where it still hung, its glory dimming day by day. I wondered whether growing such a plant was worthwhile, and then I got to thinking about Easter.

The dry waiting season of Lent ends in a blaze of glory. Easter Day is short, stunning, invigorating. The chancel is full of flowers. The pews are full of people, and everyone looks their best. Even mediocre preachers are carried away on a wave of spiritual generosity so profound that we are left wondering where that feeling is the rest of the year. The word of Easter is unabashedly about life and the clear, unmistakable power of God exhibited in the resurrection. Easter is triumph, and it is the one day on the church's calendar that is unambiguously celebrative . . . but it only blooms once a year. Like my orchid, Easter gives us one brief golden blaze of glory . . . and then sends us back to watering, waiting, and watching.

Liturgical wisdom sends us straight to the book of Acts after the glory of Easter is done for a heavy, bracing dose of what it means to do the hard work of resurrection, to *ourselves* become the body of Christ in the world, the church. Liturgically, we do this work in an in-between time—Sundays *after* Easter, and without the benefit of the Pentecost Spirit, still long weeks in coming.

The stories in the book of Acts invite us into the confusing, confirming, exhilarating world of becoming a people of God, a body for Christ, a resurrection, incarnate presence in the midst of a complicated and indifferent secular universe.

We leave the locked upper room with the fearful disciples, trembling and hoping that the *peace* Christ breathed on us with a word was real. We venture out into the world of the "Other,"—the chance-met stranger with whom sacramental bread is broken; the "Gentiles" seeking knowledge of what we have already seen and believed; the poor and forgotten on the temple steps seeking blessing; the cultured and intellectual strangers who hear our story and demand that we act on our dreams and invite them to become part of us, family—all of these opening the floodgates to a kind of chaotic, polyglot community we never imagined Jesus to have had in mind when he said, *I have other sheep who do not belong to this fold . . .*[1] We are not so much making the church as being stampeded by and into it. And when we look back, a trifle anxiously, toward the source who started us down this path in the first place, hoping for a word of guidance and counsel on the way to Jerusalem, Judea, Samaria and the uttermost parts

---

1. John 10:16, NRSV. Text for the fourth Sunday after Easter.

of the earth; suddenly it is Ascension, and he is gone, disappeared into thin air. And we are left behind, our mouths hanging open on one last, shouted question and our eyes straining for just one final glimpse, until yet *another* pair of strangers—Luke's *men dressed in white*—prod us to stop our staring and get back down to earth, so that we might get on with the work of the gospel.[2] And then next year, it all begins again!

So many variables are in play in matters of life and death—so much can and does go wrong, when the creation of a new thing is in process. When I was given the Easter orchid, I remember wondering whether, in fact, *my* orchid would actually bloom after a year at rest. Would I water it enough? Too much? Fertilize it insufficiently? *Over* fertilize it? Would the combination of sun and wind and oak tree make it possible for beauty to renew itself, or would some other place, some other combination, serve life better? All through the long, wet summer and the dry, hot fall, I did what I had been told, and tried to trust. During January and February I worried, whenever I looked at the dormant plant hanging limply outside the window. *I thought John had said it would send out little shoots of dried beadlike floral strands.* It was doing no such thing. *Easter was about this time, last year*, I thought. Maybe I had killed it off. I'm not very good with plants. When I went out to get the newspaper on the morning of the fourth Sunday of Lent (*Laetare* Sunday), I heard a bird sing and looked up at the tree, and there they were: long dried strands of pod-like beads, *the evidence of things hoped for,* as the bible says somewhere. By Easter, the golden flowers had indeed already begun to burst into life, and so I know: resurrection comes around like clockwork, whether we worry about it or not, regardless of what we do or how fretfully we prepare for the possibility of renewed life. It happens when we are not watching, but in ways unmistakable, so that we can see and make known how reliable and constant and stunning in its magnificence is the life and love of God, made visible in our midst. *Christ is risen, Alleluia.*

---

2. Acts 1:10, NRSV.

Tuning My Heart

RESISTING RESURRECTION

a meditation on the resurrection of Lazarus, John 11

Dead things stink.
Why then
roll away the stone
unbind the lengths of cloth
unfetter
expose
the hope
which had quietly lain
at rest
(if not at peace)
sealed in the shallow grave?
Quickening Spirit,
Since you will;
Speak the Word of command
that causes unquiet
Unrest
Call me—half unwilling
to the mouth of the tomb
to cringe
as one long dead
at the harsh radiance
of new life.

EASTER DAY

Mark 16:1–8   Matthew 28: 1–10

The Opposite of Certainty

What is the opposite of faith? asks the writer Anne Lamott, as she slogs through yet another day in the life—fighting with her thirteen year old son, trying to build a relationship with the boy's father, struggling with memories of her mother so bitter and angry that she cannot even bear to take the box containing her mother's ashes off of the back shelf in the guest room closet, despairing of the war in Iraq and her sense of utter impotence—as a

The Acts of Orchids

Christian believer—to make even the tiniest dent in her own hard heart, let alone in the heart of the world. *What is the opposite of faith?*[3]

Doubt is the opposite of faith. Right? Right? Only believe with all your heart, and doubts and conflicts, struggles and contradictions, will evaporate like the pre-dawn mist rising off the stone tomb of Jesus disappeared with the first rays of the sun on Easter morning.

On Easter Day of all days, it is tempting to take this way, this *via positiva*. And there are voices in scripture to help us, if this is our choice. One such story comes from the Gospel of Matthew—a Gospel with clean lines, brave conclusions, clear instructions. Dramatically supernatural, unabashedly proselytizing, Matthew's story of the resurrection is intended to leave us with no doubts.

The writer of Matthew uses every device at his disposal to convince us that the evidence of Jesus' resurrection can neither be negated nor explained away in ordinary human terms. Two earthquakes, a terrifying "angel of the Lord," all in dazzling white, the lies of the chief priests and the scribes, the myth of the stolen body . . . all are drawn forth and deployed like weapons of mass conversion to set the disciples up for lives of glittering success as they are sent out with their script and their strategic plan: *go therefore and make disciples of all nations, baptizing them in the name of the Father, Son, and Holy Spirit, and teaching them to obey everything I have commanded you . . . and lo, I am with you always, even to the end of the age*.[4]

Matthew's Gospel demonstrates the mighty acts of God in history; a certainty made visible . . . but: how can such a resurrection save *us*? We know the dark side of certainty. We are gifted with the language of power, beguiled by the winsome forcefulness of our own mythology; sure of our rights, our obligations, our mission to save the world. And yet . . . we are not reborn, and somehow, sometimes, we know it.

If freedom from doubt is the resurrection you have come seeking today, it is a buyer's market. There are Christians—and Christian communions—everywhere, who rely heavily on the power of resurrection certainty to bulldoze their way through the ordinary doubts and darknesses of daily life, the wary skepticism of people who believe differently, and the noncompliant, determined death-dealing that is life in this world among the powers and principalities. *Melt the clouds of sin and sadness, drive the*

---

3. Stories from *Plan B: Further Thoughts on Faith*, Anne Lamott.
4. Matthew 28:19–20, NRSV.

dark of doubt away, go the words of the old hymn, but in the hands of certainty, they are less a prayer than they are a militant call to arms.

The pastor of a large Presbyterian Church in Ft. Lauderdale was given nearly a full page one day this week in the op-ed section of the *Miami Herald*, offering not so much his opinion or his faith in the mystery of resurrection as he stated *just the facts, ma'am*: that the factual—the *factual* evidence of the resurrection of Jesus was so compelling, so objectively attested, so logically presented, that there was no question of "belief" at all—but rather, a universal intellectual and practical assent in the risen Christ akin to, say, knowing that Starbucks will give you a triple *venti* nonfat latte if you order it up and plunk down your $4.35.

This militant certainty that sets aside faith clears a distinct, though dangerous path through our common life: cutting a swath recently through the small community of Pinellas Park, Florida, and the little hospice where Terri Schiavo lingers in a twilight state of not-quite-living; compelling strangers—who do not know the sorrow and the struggle of her family, and who do not have the right to render judgment in this intensely private matter of life and death—to bear witness to their utter certainty that there is only one right divinely mandated choice for life, and damn to hell anyone who disagrees or doubts this action.

The *New York Times* carried in recent weeks a series of articles describing the deliberate humiliation and tormenting of Muslim captives detained at Guantanamo Bay. Hard and shameful stories, that have caused people of conscience in the military and out of it to question whether we have as a nation lost touch with our core values of tolerance and compassionate mercy. Yet more chilling, somehow, than all of these stories put together was the one reported about a soldier named Smith, who, when asked by his victim *why? why are you tormenting me?* replied simply *because I am a Christian.*

The opposite of faith is not, as we have been programmed to believe, doubt.

The opposite of faith is certainty.

Me, I do not do so well with certainty these days. The fixed script seems rigid, unyielding. The formula does not fit the fabric of life unfolding around me, around the people in the spiritual community I call home. In the face of brokenness, doubt, and fragility; in the midst of hard questions with no easy answers; in the stillness of a hospice room where Terri Schiavo lies dying while her family fights and prays for clarity, for truth, and for mercy; in Red Lake, Minnesota, where shattered families and a violated Native American tribal community are listening for answers and gathering up the tangled threads of violence, alienation and death; in these lengthening, soul-draining days of war; in the small potent tragedies of families and individuals that cause us to clear our throats and lift up our small voices in prayer, week after week . . . *Lord, hear our prayer.*

What does it mean to make a disciple? What is the purpose of our baptism? How does the meaning of Christ's resurrection—so clear inside the small world of the ancient gospel witness, so difficult to touch and grasp in the hard light of day—really have the potential to transform us? Does it?

The ending of the Gospel of Mark—which no observant person would dare to call a "resurrection story"—is, as we receive it, singularly lacking in miracle, almost devoid of hope, and ridiculously lacking in role models, populated as it is by an ambiguous "man in white" and frightened, silent women who, even when commanded, cannot muster a word of witness to contradict the looming emptiness of the silent tomb.

But what if the subtle scent of resurrection has been overshadowed by our cheap dependence upon the trappings of power and certainty? What if faith flowers there, and here, in the *midst* of the doubt and the fear, instead of being badgered into existence by relentless constructions of creeds and demands?

The words at the close of the Gospel of Mark that describe the reactions of the women who went to the empty tomb are generally translated in the most unflattering and destructive of ways: they were "alarmed." They were overcome by "fear," "trembling" in terror—they said nothing to anyone because they were "afraid."

But I believe it is the culture of Certainty that devalues the unique and tender witness of the women who went to the tomb of Jesus in the Gospel of Mark. There is ample textual evidence to suggest an alternative translation, one that honors the nuances of fear, doubt, and struggle that pave our pathways to grace, and at the same time affirms that resurrection is possible *not* in spite of, but *because of* our attentiveness to uncertainty, doubt, and mystery. Listen: *And going out they fled the tomb, for trembling and ecstasy possessed them, and they said nothing to anyone, for they were filled with awe.*[5]

5. Mark 16:8, author's rendering, based on the work of Marie Noonan Sabin in *Reopening the Word: Reading Mark as Theology in the Context of Early Judaism.*

I have been thinking that this year is for me, an Alligator Easter. Let me explain.

My friend Eric, a psychotherapist specializing in traumatic stress, suggests that when we are frightened or have experienced trauma, our thinking, spiritual selves go into "fight or flight" mode. We lose the ability to think, to explore creative options, and we reduce everything to the certainty that we must kill or be killed. My friend calls this being possessed by our "alligator brain," and we have all been there and done that. You know what I mean . . . whether your experience is the profound terror of a life threatening attack or accident . . . or the more mundane—but no less alarming—experience of someone with power over us threatening our well being; financially, professionally, emotionally. Confronted with terror and threat, our certainty is fixed, and our choices are two: kill it and eat it, or run away, so it does not eat you. A world of infinite possibilities dissolves into the orthodoxy of fear, of violence. Our god-given creativity and imagination is smothered by threat. Eric counsels that if we can only be aware that this is our primitive response, we can be in charge of it, and change it. We can sense our body's tightening, feel the adrenaline that cuts off our reason, and choose not to be controlled by it. Accepting our fear, our distress, we can breathe, relax our bodies, free our mind—and soul—to explore alternatives with creativity, courage, and grace. The key thing is to breathe, and to know that *we* are the ones who choose whether to die to our higher self, our soul, or to be born again.

This is how it is in the "resurrection story" that closes the Gospel of Mark . . . there is fear, and doubt, and the power to choose not to run away, but to stay with it, so that something new might begin to do its work in the women . . . or in us.

When our devotion to a "faith" grounded in certainty tempts us, the witness of the silent women in Mark calls us instead to a way of believing that is open ended, unfinished. A way of believing that acknowledges that God's revelation is always born in mystery, and worked out in our bodies through our attentive, mindful participation in all of life's experiences, mundane and extraordinary alike.

When we are tempted by a belief system that calls upon us to march off into a world of absolute assertions that trample people's rights and impose a tyranny of certainty upon ourselves and others—especially when we are facing hard times and difficult choices—the women of Mark suggest that running off half-cocked from the empty tomb to babble whatever it is we think we *know*, is at best a useless expense of effort, and at worst, an arrogance that tramples the fragile flowers that bloom in the fertile soil of suffering and doubt.

If we are longing for a strategic Christian plan of decisive, prescribed action, we might try instead the discipleship of the women of Mark, who practice their watchfulness at the crucifixion and a mindfulness at the empty tomb that acknowledges that God's revealing of godself is more in the ordinary than in the spectacular or miraculous.

Mark's Gospel invites anyone who comes to comprehend that they—that we—are made in God's image, and therefore are capable of reflecting God in the world.

Is this not what the *other* Christian "Smith," Ashley Smith of Atlanta, showed us when she, a wounded soul in search of saving grace, encountered another broken child of God, the fugitive Brian Nichols, who had raped and killed and fled justice in a nationally televised manhunt two weeks ago? Taken prisoner in her own home, Ashley confronted her terror and reached into the empty tomb of doubt for grace. Like wisdom in the Proverbs, like God in the Psalms, like Christ on the cross, she set a table for her enemy, and found a brother. She listened to his story of failure and pain, and shared her own, and in the breaking of bread and hearts, the mystery of resurrection was made flesh.

In Greek, the Gospel of Mark ends with a preposition, "gar," which means *for*. As we all know, ending a sentence with a preposition is sloppy, incomplete, and leading—which is all a gospel should be, everything a resurrection might become, if we let it.

Our trembling is not terror—but holy awe, that in every circumstance, God is doing a new thing . . . if we will allow ourselves to participate in it.

Our speechlessness is not less, but more than words . . . as we consider not what we *are* sure of, but what we are not . . . which is where God is bringing a new thing to life, an eloquent silence that is an open space in which we might write the resurrection's meaning for ourselves.

Tuning My Heart

EASTER DAY

Luke 24:1-11

The Green Flash

Some years ago, when I stood in the uncertain space
between childhood and adolescence
I remember reading a note at the bottom of a page of the
    Reader's Digest
It described something called *the Green Flash.*

The Green Flash was something that happened at deep dawn,[6]
at the dark edge of day,
a moment before the sun burst over the horizon.
If you went out in the darkness of night
and could see the horizon clearly
and waited patiently,
just before the sun rose over the edge of the world
you would see it
a green flash,
momentary, ephemeral.
A glorious sign of the mystery of Light.
The article said you could see it best on the East Coast, by the ocean.

I lived in the northern Midwest, in the midst of a forest.
There was not much of a horizon
And besides, I disliked the cold darkness of early morning,
much preferring the full light of day.

I still do.
Deep dawn is the time when the telephone rings,
and in the dark, you are confused, fumbling
lost
and the news is never good.
There have been too many deep dawns lately.
And no green flash.

---

6. The phrase is borrowed from James Lowry, in the *Journal for Preachers*, Easter, 2004.

The Acts of Orchids

In the bible,
only the gospel of Luke describes the time when the women came to the tomb
early on the first day of the week
as "deep dawn."

Matthew says the first day was dawning.
Mark says it was very early
John says it was still dark . . .

But Luke has his unnamed women
go to anoint the body of their dead friend
in the sad, lost hour
of deep dawn.

I think I know why he said it that way.

For me
for many of us
this year—this *week*—
has been a season of deep dawn.

An endless moment of gray
When you strain to see through the shadows
for the hope of morning
and wonder
whether to believe that the sun will ever rise

This year,
in the deep dawn of this holy week,
I believe I have begun to understand
    for the first time
that believing in the promise of the resurrection
  is, even for the devout Christian,
  really a *choice,*
  not an inevitability
  nor an article of faith.

Tuning My Heart

The world
Circumstances—
    are giving us many alternative choices.

We can believe the angels' promise
that there will be *peace on earth, good will among men*
Or we can read the news
Watch CNN and the reports from
Fallujah, Palestine, Israel . . .
    Remember Darfur.

We can listen to the messengers in white who greet us
    do not be afraid
    and who tell us *he is risen.*
Or we can answer the phone at deep dawn and listen to
    the unrecognizable voice of someone we love
choke out the hardest words in the world
    he's gone.
There are times in which it is easy to believe the good news of the gospel
and other times
    when the defense of disbelieving
makes a good deal more sense
    and feels safer
        seeming to protect us from a world of disappointment and hurt.

When you come right down to it
there never has been any proof of the resurrection
    not even in this story of Luke's
where the women come
and they are surprised by the messengers
who said, *he is not here...*

but what they meant was,
    you have a choice
    you can go back and say "he is gone . . . "
    or you can Remember what he said
    and choose to believe instead
    that he is risen.

I saw a movie recently called *Secondhand Lions.*

The Acts of Orchids

It concerned a young boy,
    abandoned by his mother
    left to spend the summer alone
        on a dusty farm in the hill country of Texas
    with his two isolated, supposedly rich
    strange and unfriendly great uncles.
That boy didn't choose to trust anybody
    and with good reason.
During the course of the summer,
    one of the uncles began to tell the story of their lives...
a fantastic story of adventure and derring-do
    a story of riches, companionship, and true love
It seemed unbelievable
    but then the boy found bags full of money
        buried under the barn.

The neighbors all believed the brothers were bank robbers.
    So did his mother.

So the boy asked his uncles
    these stories ... they're true, aren't they?
And the uncle said,
    it doesn't matter.
But the boy responded fiercely
    It does matter.
    All I hear from my mother are lies.
    I need the truth.

And the uncle said, *no,*
    you need to hear my speech.
Sometimes the things that may or may not be true
    are the things a man needs to believe in the most
That people are basically good.
That there is honor, courage, and virtue
    in everything
And good always triumphs over evil... and,
    I want you to remember this—

Tuning My Heart

Love,
true love,
never dies.
A man has to choose what to believe.

Later that summer,
    in the hours of deep dawn,
    the boy woke up to the sound of a car
    and his mother whispering,
did you find the money?
Hurry, let's go . . .
I've come to take you away to a good life.
They're bank robbers,
    The money is as much ours as anybody's
    And they don't deserve it.

The boy tried to tell his mother
    they weren't bank robbers, but adventurers
    whose wealth was the gift of
        a grateful sheik whose life they had redeemed.

But the mother shook her son
    Mr. Doubting Thomas,
    Surely you don't believe that Africa crap
    Do you?
And the boy stood for a minute
    in the darkness and dust
    of his uncles' yard
    and looked at his mother's face in the shadows
and it was deep dawn
and the boy's face was screwed up in concentration
    and in the wary fear of being duped
        again
And suddenly he relaxed
    and raised his head
    and Remembered what his uncle had said
And he told his mother fiercely

    Yes

The Acts of Orchids

    Yes I do believe.

He had to make a choice
    for the boy he had been shaped to be
    or for the man he wanted to become
He chose love.

We have to make a choice as well.
    to believe the evidence of death
    and violence
    and shoddy, shallow selfishness
that is all around us...
And to protect ourselves accordingly
    as best we can
        through cynicism
        self-protection
        and tending to the business of saving ourselves
            and those we love...

Or we can believe the resurrection
    even though we have never seen it
    and the shadows are dense over the faces
        of those who wait in the deep darkness with us...

If we choose to believe
    we need to Remember.
We need to remember what Jesus said.

On Wednesday of this past week,
    I was by myself at home
typing the bulletin for Buddy's memorial service
I was angry and sad.
Even before Buddy died on Tuesday
I had already been,
    for a number of reasons many of you know already,
    dreading the onset of Easter...
        for which I felt unusually ill-prepared spiritually

Usually I have no trouble choosing to believe

Tuning My Heart

  but this year of death and loss has been difficult
    and the choosing has been hard

While I was typing the bulletin
  I remembered
It would be Maundy Thursday when we remembered Norman
  And so that is what I wrote:
Celebrating the Life of Norman Eugene "Buddy" Bliss,
Maundy Thursday
April 8, 2004.

One of the family members from out of town
  and several of the retired FBI agents
  who came to the service
  pulled me aside
Asking,
  What is this word, "Maundy?"
  What is Maundy Thursday?

And I remembered, and told them . . .
  It comes from the Latin "mandate"
  It means commandment.

What commandment? they said
And I remembered.
I remembered what Jesus said,
I am giving you a new commandment
  that you love one another
    as I have loved you . . .
  that you also love one another.
And I told them.
And I also told them that that is how I believe Norman lived his life among us.

And suddenly,
  Choosing to believe in resurrection,
   In Easter . . .
    didn't seem so impossible any more.

All through this long year of war and turmoil

> of personal loss
> and deep wounds in my own life
> and in the life of many people in this community of
> faith I love
> It has seemed that my reserves have been draining away
> my hope struggling to survive
> in the midst of a deep dawn kind of darkness that never was
> going to
> see the green flash
>
> But I saw it Good Friday morning
> when I woke up and knew that my choice had been made
> My choice to believe had been made
> because I remembered what Jesus said,
> and I saw how you remembered it, too.
>
> Did you notice that Luke never names the people
> who went to the tomb
> and believed without evidence
> and told the others he was risen
> He never names them at all until the very end of the story?
>
> Now I'm at the end of *my* story, and I will name them, as well:
> It's you.
> the people of Riviera
> not each of you alone . . .
> but all of you, together, a small but holy community
> telling with your lives
> that you remember what Jesus said
> and you are trying to live it.
>
> You take in small foster children, nurture them into health, then let
> them go.
> You experience miscarriages, divorces, losses of livelihood, illness
> you grieve the deaths of people you love,
> and endure the slow slipping of old friends into confusion or
> infirmity
> But you don't stop choosing to believe
> And you don't stop showing up

Tuning My Heart

And you come to church,
    Sunday after Sunday
        And you pray and remember and believe
    And you go out into your own worlds and you live it there
And then you come back and do it all over again.

You were at the door for Alice on Tuesday
    on the phone, the computer
There were flowers
    food and stories
        offers of assistance of every kind
            hugs, tears, laughter
And you will be there the next time,
    when it is someone else's turn . . .

You know that Christ is Risen,
    because you, the community of his people here
    are remembering what he said
    and living what he told us to do.

He is risen
    is not an assertion to be made by one's self
    getting through an individual life as best one can
        waiting alone in the deep dawn
            hoping not to blink
                lest I miss the moment of the green flash . . .

He is risen
    is about community
    loving one another as Christ loved us
    being each other's eyes
    arms
    legs
    hearts. . .
believing for one another
    when one cannot believe alone
        because the others
            and the scoffing world
        say that it is only an idle tale.

The Acts of Orchids

It is not an idle tale—
   Not "idle" at all,
      but a work in progress.
   The work of the people of Christ
   the work of Love
   the work of choosing to believe
      even in the deep dawn
   that we have been
      and even now are being
   delivered out of darkness…
      and into resurrection light.

Amen, and Amen.

LOW SUNDAY

Exodus 14

Nahshon's Story

A midrash is an interpretative "take" on a biblical text, a teaching and exegetical practice used in the Jewish tradition. On the Sunday after Easter one year, tired of the "faithful few" feeling Low Sunday let-down, we left the sanctuary to the dying Easter lilies, and convened our "faithful few" around a constructed table similar to the one we had celebrated communion around on Maundy Thursday. The service, including both the celebration of the Eucharist and the sharing of a simple soup luncheon, was meant to evoke the presence of the post-Easter disciples, gathered in the upper room, trying to find in the sharing of stories (a Passover tradition) the courage and the strength to go on without the living Jesus among them. The service included confession, prayer, song, scripture, and storytelling. I wrote this story as a tribute to the every-Sunday Christians who get the job done, proclaiming the gospel with their lives, sometimes in the face of overwhelming difficulties and resistance, always imaginatively. Here is that Sunday-after-Easter midrash on a traditional Jewish midrash concerning Nahshon, the man who walked alone into the Red Sea so that the waters could part, and the Hebrew slaves escape the pursuing Egyptians.

We were used to doing what we were told. Four hundred years of slavery—well, it ingrains a life-long habit, difficult to break. It was our life, and our survival. Listening. Obeying. Anticipating the next command—anything to avoid the lash. An enslaved people—especially those who have been slaves so long they have forgotten what it meant to be free—specialize in invisibility. We do not stand out from the crowd. We do not get caught alone. We do not draw attention to ourselves. We do what we are told.

As I said, we were used to it, we believed our lives depended on it—and such habits are hard to break. We cannot say we were not warned—when Moses came, he told us how it would be different for us, when we would be free; but still, it was impossible to imagine what being "free" might mean. Even when Moses told us how it had been for him—how, after years of fleeing and hiding, after disappearing so entirely into the colorless life of a nomad shepherd in Midian, the Voice called *him* to step out, to step into the holy circle where the Light of God was burning, burning without being consumed, and he was afraid. Afraid, he was, even Moses, the Prince of Egypt, because the habit of hiding had become second nature, even for him. He told us how, drawn by that strange fire, the voice bade him—take *off your shoes, this is holy ground*. And he remembered—in the old language, the language before slavery, the command meant this: not *take off your shoes*, but *change your habits*. Live a different way. And he understood the voice to be saying, the time for hiding and isolation was done. So Moses left his flocks behind, and returned to Egypt—to us—to confront his fears, his failures, and to face down the might of Pharaoh, so that we all could be free.

Even then, we did not get it. And truthfully, the habit of doing what we were told held us in good stead, much of the way. Moses said we must be ready to flee, and so we were. Moses said we must anoint the lintels of our doors with blood, and so we did. Moses said we must not plan for time for bread to rise, but must pack our treasures, our families, and food for the journey, and be ready ... and so we were.

See, the habits of slaves are difficult to break. And whether it was one man or another giving the orders scarcely mattered to us. It seemed an adventure, almost, leaving Egypt—but hardly the start of a new way of life. A pillar of cloud by day, of fire by night. A different place, a different master, new orders. Our part—obeying—stayed just the same.

Doing what we were told, we were saved from the angel of death, protected from the anger of Pharaoh, and brought to the brink of safety with our wives and our children and our livestock, to the banks of the Red Sea, where, Moses had said, the god who spoke out of fire and blood, who hovered in cloud and flame, would open a way through the waters that we might be saved.

And so we waited there, for this miracle of the Red Sea.

At first, there was no fear, only a kind of feast-day frenzied feeling . . . we had obeyed Moses and his invisible god—and, obeying, had got away—safe out of Egypt! We thought we had time. Huddling together as much out of habit as need, we waited, and watched Moses the master as he watched the sea. And watched it.

Hours passed, or was it days? The pillar of flame flickered and went out. The cloud that rose behind us had nothing to do with any god we wanted to know. The loud, joyous conversations slid into whispers, and the bold glances at the sea before us and at vanished, vanquished Egypt behind us faltered, changed to downcast eyes. And what we heard on the breeze was no longer the laughing cry of sea birds flying overhead, but the thunder of chariots far off, and the shouts of angry men.

Moses waited, and watched, his staff cast before him on the sand.

The rest of us—slaves still, and soon perhaps again—sat restive and increasingly afraid. We had heard it whispered that Moses had called upon the god to fight for us, and God had spoken in reply, *why are you crying to Me? Tell the children of Israel to go forward.*

We were ready to follow orders—more than ready. But none came, and there was silence by the edge of the sea, silence and the stirring of the rising storm at our heels.

"Abba, what should we do now?" It was the voice of my middle child, small, inquisitive Raisa, whom I had not seen since the Egyptian lady took her away to be maidservant to her eldest daughter months ago. "Abba, do something."

But what was to be done? I was good only for following orders, and none had been given. I looked up—no one, not even Moses, caught my eyes. Sitting by himself, back against a rock, he seemed lost in memory— or maybe, just lost.

No one moved, no one spoke. The only eyes lifted to meet my own were the brown, trusting eyes of my daughter, still waiting for an answer, a possibility, a beginning. The thunder of horses grew louder, and dust clouds rose on the near horizon.

I looked out toward the sea. The sun danced across the water, lighted the wave tops with flame, caught, and then held. The sea was burning, burning with a holy fire that neither went out, nor was consumed. Without thinking, I rose to my feet, kicked off my sandals, moved across the wet sand and into the shallow edge of the sea. I shook off the hands that tried to restrain me. Unbidden, a voice seemed to speak in my head: t*his, too, is holy ground. Nahshon, it is your time to change a habit now.* I waded deeper, not listening to the shouts of wonder from my fellow slaves, the frantic orders from Moses and Aaron. *Wait!* they said, *come back!* It seemed to take a long time, a lifetime. I knew the time for following orders was past, and as the water reached my nostrils, I understood that the slave habit had been broken forever, and that whatever happened, I was free. A huge wave set me sputtering, stumbling to my knees. When it passed, there were shouts again—my neighbor, my daughter—and suddenly, they were all around me, pushing, running, catching me up under my arms and shaking me loose from the waters in which I lay, face down . . . the waters that now, stretching as far as the eye could see, were no deeper than a child's footprint in the sand, no more menacing than a tear.

The rest, you know. We crossed the Red Sea on dry land, and when we reached the other side, Miriam and the women danced and sang for joy—"Sing to the Lord, for God has triumphed gloriously! The horse and rider thrown into the sea." But we knew that God's triumph that day had little to do with the horsemen of Egypt, and everything to do with taking that first step on the holy ground of choosing to be free.

EASTERTIDE

Acts 8:26-40

In Over Our Heads

The unlikely subject of this strange little evangelistic encounter in the Acts of the Apostles was a foreigner, a Gentile, a black man, and a eunuch: a man physically mutilated in order to neutralize his sexuality, making him a fit servant for the queen of the Ethiopians. And Philip?—well, let Philip stand for someone a lot like one of us . . . a person trying to be faithful to the way of Jesus; a believer trying to make sense of his faith in the midst of a confusing and chaotic world. A person belonging to a religious tradition—Judaism—that had pretty strict rules about who could and could not be a part of the community of God.

Though the telling of it is matter of fact, make no mistake: Philip, obeying the Spirit's direction, was in a tight spot—a theologically indefensible position. Even the rare and miraculous experience of sensing himself visited by an angel of the Lord must have paled into insignificance when Philip saw just whom it was God had sent him to save. Indeed, a heavenly vision would have been easier to believe than this: the reception into the kingdom of God of a man completely unsuitable, unfit, for membership in the covenant community. What would Philip say to the synagogue? Where could he go for support, when law and custom in Israel had named that unnamed Ethiopian unfit, outcast, "not my people?"

Foreigners and Gentiles were outsiders, unfamiliar with the ways of Israel, and their involvement with the Jewish faith was strictly regulated. Even those who worshipped the God of Israel, called "God-fearers," were kept at arm's length: there was for them a separate-but-equal place in worship, an outside court on the fringe of the temple called the Court of the Gentiles. Conversion into the Jewish faith was no easy matter: the practice of the day called for rabbis to reject the proselyte three separate times before considering him for conversion to Judaism. Philip was no rabbi; the conditions for conversion could not possibly be met on a lonely desert road. And if that were not enough, the man was a eunuch as well—and the Bible was clear about those kinds of people. The legal code in Deuteronomy strictly prohibited those whose sexual organs were mutilated from even setting foot on the temple grounds, let alone becoming part of the faith.

The fact is, the struggling young movement could ill afford such controversy. The followers of the Christ were still Jews, generally bound by the conventions of Israel, and they wanted it that way. The church thought of itself as Jewish, lived as a Jewish minority community. It could not conceive of what it might mean to be cut off from the history and tradition of their faith. Moreover, the infant church needed the protection of Judaism: as part of a tolerated religion in the Roman Empire, the people of Christ were safe; but if they were to be cut off, they would be unprotected, exposed to terrifying persecution.

But accept into the faith this foreigner, this eunuch?—and the community's very position and place in the community of Israel would be at risk. Would it be worth it, for Philip and the church, to lose everything for the sake of one rich Ethiopian Eunuch?

But there's one more thing I need to tell you about Philip—and this one is important—he was a Jew, and a follower of Jesus, true: yet he was also a man who could be described as an *inside-outsider*: a person who belonged to a tradition, yet who, because of his background, and his schooling, and the cultural environment in which he was brought up, just didn't quite see things the way most of the *real* insiders saw them. Philip (you can tell by his name) was a Hellenistic Jew—one of those folks whose ancestors, following the return from exile of the Jewish people, had been influenced more by the liberal, cosmopolitan tradition of the Greek Empire than by the parochial, narrow outlook of the Jerusalem returnees from Babylon. As Jerusalem was rebuilt, the stories in the biblical books of Ezra and Nehemiah tell us, the leadership of the community suggested that the way to a strong national identity was to be found in racial, cultural, and religious purity. But Greek-influenced Jews—the Hellenists—believed that the future of the Jewish people could be better served through openness to the world's cultures and a broader tradition of inclusion. So, Philip's people had —for three hundred years—existed as part of the Jewish community, but always on the fringe, because their progressive ideas and open-minded practices made them different from mainstream practitioners of the tradition.

In an age of divisive struggle in churches of all denominations over social, theological, and practical issues, this will read less like Scripture, and more like family history for those of us who commonly identify with the progressive margins of the church of Jesus Christ. We share with Philip a concern regarding what might happen to the church if we examine the book and look at the rules in new ways; and we share with Philip the knowledge that our choices will affect people for whom Christ died: people on the outside, the eunuchs and the outcasts of our day who want to be accepted by the church; and people on the inside as well, who love the church and are afraid of the changes that may hurt her or transform her into something they cannot recognize.

But we here on the Caribbean edge of America also share with Philip one more wonderful and freeing characteristic—a history and an immersion in a cultural world so diverse, so exciting and challenging, that we simply cannot close the windows and the doors and pretend we are alone in the universe. We share with Philip a need—and at last, I hope, a desire, to see where the Spirit of God will take us in the world . . . and we share with him a conviction that God is in the midst of us, no matter how strange or unfamiliar the road we tread.

We have been further gifted by the Spirit with the imagination to seek throughout the scriptures and deep into the tradition for those words and those happenstances that remind us how good, how broad, and how universal the love of God truly is.

Whom does Philip see, when he climbs aboard that chariot at the urging of some Spirit of newness he cannot ignore? A foreigner, a mutilated man, a seeker after grace? He sees all of this, yes, and then he sees, as well, the page of Scripture to which this enigmatic Ethiopian has turned. *As a sheep led to the slaughter or a lamb before the shearers is dumb, so he does not open his mouth. In his humiliation justice was denied him. Who will ever see his descendents? For his life has been taken up from the earth.*[7] *About whom,* the eunuch gently inquires, *does the prophet say this? About himself, or about someone else?*[8]

And Philip looked up, and saw before him not a stranger, but someone just like the one whom the prophet described. A eunuch, who quietly went to his mutilation because he was destined to be slave to the queen. A man for whom the simple justice of choosing his own way and his own life would be forever denied him. A man whose descendents would never be seen, because other people had determined that they could never be born. A man unwelcome in the house of Israel. A man who despite all of that, was still drawn in love, in painful yearning, to the heart of a religion, which by its own rules could never accept him.

Philip saw all of that, and then in that black man's face and in his own, and in the open pages of Scripture, he saw the face of someone else—the risen stranger who had warned his disciples *I am with you always.* And seeing that one, he opened his mouth and beginning with that Scripture, told the good news of Jesus the outcast, in whose love and in whose name Philip found an opportunity to embrace one more outsider whom God loved.

Look, here is water! What is to prevent me from being baptized?[9]

Here is water. This week, our Jewish neighbors are celebrating the Passover—the festival of liberation from slavery in the land of Egypt. It

---

7. Isaiah 53:7–8, RSV.
8. Acts 8:34, NRSV.
9. Acts 8:37, NRSV.

is a festival that is rooted in water—the parted waters of the Red Sea. I want to offer you a lesson shared with my by a rabbi friend of mine earlier this week. He tells me that in Hebrew, the word "Egypt" is rendered Mitzrayim—the literal translation for which is "twice narrow." That Egypt is, he says, the "straightjacket of history"—where kings spent their entire lives building their graves.

The life of Egypt, the life of slavery, can be understood as a life of unbearable narrowness. When the Israelites fled slavery, they found themselves pursued by the Egyptians to the banks of the Red Sea. There, with the roiling waters before them, and Pharaoh with the army of death behind them and gaining; the community turns on Moses in accusation: *were there not enough graves in Egypt that you have taken us to the wilderness to die?*

A midrash—a traditional rabbinical commentary—says of this passage: *when the tribes stood at the sea, this one said, 'I'm not going in first,' and that one said, 'I'm not going in first.' And as they were arguing, Nahshon, son of Aminadav, leapt into the sea.* And when he did, the water of the sea parted, and Israel was saved as the people walked across on dry land. A leader, said my friend, is a person who finds a way of hope through the water, rather than standing around arguing why it can't be done. This is our job, the job of inside-outsiders, the job of followers of Jesus the Galilean. In our own community this very day, there are a host of people—and potent issues of immigration, race, poverty, and war; and someone, for the love of God, must be first to step into the waters—so that God can part them, and the people can be saved.

Here is water! What is to prevent my being baptized?

What, indeed? The rules and the tradition may seem to speak with one voice—but the Spirit of God that parts the waters of death speaks in another—a voice sometimes heavily accented, sometimes strange—but nevertheless, a voice that is familiar, because it is rooted and grounded in the deepest waters of all: the waters where the love of God moves and breathes and brings life out of chaos. Those are the waters in which we swim, this small community of followers of the way of Jesus—and these are the waters in which we may be buried with Christ and raised to a new life. In a place not too far from here, on a day not too long ago, a very traditional presbytery spoke the church's will for a people they considered not their own, our gay and lesbian brothers and sisters, who continue to try to serve the church they love as God has called them. At the end of that vote, when the denomination once again said *NO* to inclusion; one of those people, call him *Philip*, if you will, stood with a foot in the door of the temple that had just banished him: *Jesus loves me,* he sang in a clear, proud voice, *this I know, for the Bible tells me* so.

Fellow members of the family of the evangelist Philip, and Jesus' own beloved ones, may we proclaim our own faith in the same song, and make it this time, a new song:

> *Jesus loves me, this I know; for the bible tells me so.*
> *Little ones to him belong, they are weak, but he is strong.*
> *Yes, Jesus loves me! Yes, Jesus loves me! Yes, Jesus loves me,*
> *The Bible tells me so.*

EASTERTIDE

Acts 9:36–43

Saints and Widows

When the Oklahoma City bomber, Timothy McVeigh, died, his execution was watched by the families of his victims on closed circuit television.

Some of them believed his death would give them closure.

Others believed it gave him satisfaction: the knowledge that his life made
    a difference.

I wonder. I wonder as I listened, and watched, and read the debate about the publicizing of his death. Vengeance? Justice? Deterrence?

No one seems sure, really, how the memorial made of Timothy McVeigh's dying will serve the common good ... or if it will.

This concerns me. Though what concerns me more is why—
Why the living and the dying of this man matters more, somehow, than the unremarked living and dying of one, of a thousand saints known only to a few, whose lives *really* made a difference: whose living brought light to the world.

It gives me hope, then, to read in the bible this morning—
To read how Luke interrupts his headlong dash through the explosive expansion of the early church in the book of Acts long enough to notice the death of one otherwise unremarked widow,
    the woman Tabitha
Why do our lives matter?

The evangelist Luke has a tendency to be dismissive about the women in
his church. Even in this story, this story about the woman Tabitha, called
Dorcas.
He calls the men "saints" and "disciples," but the women, merely
   "widows."
As if women who had the misfortune of being left behind matter too little
   to name
   Even to name "saint."
We know people like this. People too big, too busy, too distracted
   to notice the little lives around them.
   or the ones who regard their own lives as of little consequence
To themselves, they are not "saints,"
   merely, something else, beneath Naming—
   existing in the category "Other."
But there is something about this woman Tabitha Luke can't dismiss.
Something that forced him to call her a title reserved in his lexicon,
   exclusively for the most significant of men: he calls her Disciple.
She is a leader in her community—*extremely generous,* Luke says.
A woman of wealth and influence, a woman who provided for her whole
community not just alms—but clothing in abundance, crafted with love
and skill.
   A most personal gift for those Others, those "widows,"
     beneath Naming.
Tabitha knew their names.
   Tabitha, Dorcas, a woman at home in a cosmopolitan city,
gracefully spanning the Greek and Hebrew worlds,
making a home and a haven for all, in both worlds . . .
No wonder the women wept, and the men sent for Peter.
No wonder Luke had no other name for such a woman except Disciple.
No wonder they stood, tears streaming down their faces, while spilling
   from their hands
were garments of linen, of wool, embroidered, plain—
Their abundance and craftsmanship mute testimony to the value
   Of the life that had been lost.
Peter, seeing it all, was, Luke implies, himself overcome—
How do you measure the meaning of a life? How do you count its loss?
Peter sent the women from the room—not, I think, because he expected
   a miracle

but because he had nothing to offer in the face of their pain.
Collapsing at her bedside . . . he allowed himself to think—
    He sought a word, a spirit of comfort from God.
Images flashed
    Tabitha, welcoming the disciples to her home . . .
There was always enough food.
    A child, dressed in a gown Tabitha had made, glowing with pride as
she lifted her face for the water of baptism.
    A poor man, rags discarded, clothed in sturdy homespun,
standing straighter, his dignity restored.
Extra food, slipped onto the church's common table—always without a
    word.
Packets made up and slipped into the bundles of the widows who were
    too proud to beg,
    but whom, everyone knew, had too little to live on.
Only Tabitha noticed enough to care.
Some of them, Peter realized,
He had just herded from the room without a thought for their own grief.
With shame he thought *I don't even know their names. But she did, every one.*
Head bowed, he vowed to change his life. To honor their lost friend
    as the widows—
    rather, as the *women,* the *disciples* downstairs did
To open himself to the poor,
To live less provincially, more generously, more openly.
To offer less of words and more of himself.
Determined now, his sense of despair and loss began to lift,
    And a new hope, a bigger world, different than before,
      Rose within him.
Yes, he would honor Tabitha's life by letting the Christ presence
    So evident in her
Break him open, spill out as he knew it longed to do,
Disregarding the limits and the lessons of prudence and law.
So that no one would ever be dismissed,
    Disregarded by him ever again.
He thought about the invitation he had just received from that tanner—
    Who was it? Yes, Simon was his name, too—
Whom he had resolved for the sake of ritual purity to shun—
And determined in a moment of reckless daring that he,

That he, Simon Peter, would for Christ's sake, for Tabitha's,
    Open up his world, push boundaries aside.
He would go gladly and stay at the tanner's home,
    gladly go *anywhere* he might be invited in Christ's name.
Peter moved to stand, eager to tell the women that he understood now
    What they had been trying to say.
    She would live on in them, and in him, too.
He rose, and in the bed before him the dead woman stirred.
Tabitha, get up, he said, and his voice shook with joy
    as hand in hand, they descended the stair
    Two disciples, a widow and a man
Descending like the Spirit of God, incarnate
Rising like the Christ spirit out of their separate tombs
    of indifference, of death.
Moving to reclaim their empty chairs at the Table of New Life.
    May the Christ Presence,
In whose name *we* this day come to keep the feast,
    Dwell in us for good,
And cause us by grace, to do the same. Amen, amen.

ASCENSION SUNDAY

Acts 1:1-11   *Luke 24:44-53*

Rites of Passage

God has gone up with a merry shout, sang the choir a few minutes ago, commemorating this Sunday of the Ascension. Contemplating that text last week, I confess I was more than bemused by the image those words evoked, the disconcerting picture of God laughing as he disappears, inexplicably, from our sight. But this morning, hearing the words again, my heart instead is flooded with memory. There were thousands of us seated in uncomfortable folding chairs on the lawn in the chill of a late spring morning. The sun, making a valiant effort to rise over the towering chestnut trees flanking the commons, cast a warming glow over the tents to our left, but we had been sitting already for hours, and we were cold, and bored. Few of us could see the stage at the end of the long field, but the sound system was good, and all of us could hear. A festival spirit prevailed, as those in the back of the crowd chatted with their relatives, made brief forays to the bookstore, and passed around cups of steaming coffee and bags of doughnuts. As the morning wore on, there were scattered flurries of activity from various points around the green, and intermittent shouts began to penetrate the droning voice being projected from the far end of the field.

Margarita G. Morales, the voice intoned, and a whoop of joy went up from a clot of folks sitting a hundred yards down and to my right. *Adam Edward Natysin*—another shriek from somewhere behind me—and then, suddenly, it was our turn: *Aimee Patricia Neale,* he said, and we were on our feet, arms waving, throats opening in a mighty, united, joyful cry, and then, in a few minutes, graduation was over.

There are two different stories that describe the event the church calls "the Ascension of Jesus Christ." One of them ends the Gospel of Luke, and the other opens the book of Acts. Oddly enough, though they were written by the same hand, they are strikingly different stories, both in content and in feel. In the last verses of Luke, in his first "take" on the ascension of Jesus, the risen Christ takes great pains to thoroughly prepare his disciples for their new life as leaders of the church following his departure. *He* opened *their minds to understand the scriptures;* he reminded them of *everything* he had taught them; *he led them out; he blessed them.*[10] There is a satisfying feeling of completion in this story—as if, despite the fact that Jesus must go, he has taken great pains to adequately prepare them for their new life: fitted them so well, in fact, for their independence that even as he disappears (though, actually, in Luke he more tactfully "withdraws") the disciples are so filled with strength, with conviction, with resources for the future, that they scarcely seem to mind his departure—I mean, his "withdrawal" at all: *and they worshipped him, and returned to Jerusalem with great joy, and were continually in the Temple blessing God.*[11] *God has gone up with a mighty shout*—and, it seems, everyone feels wonderful about the entire thing.

But in the beginning of the book of Acts, our writer seems to have had a change of heart . . . and the disciples, again poised to repeat the scene of Jesus' ascension into heaven, have had a definite change of mood.

The joy is gone.

---

10. Luke 24:45–50, NRSV.
11. Luke 24:52, NRSV.

The blessing is gone. The soft lighting has given way to the harsh glare of an unforgiving sun, into which the suddenly bereaved disciples are squinting as they struggle to get a last, good look at the disappearing Jesus. His last words to them were not blessing, but almost a rebuke—*it is not for you to know the times or seasons,* he said, and just as they were preparing to ask yet another of their important, pressing questions—he disappeared from their sight—*snap*—just like that.[12]

There is almost a fed-up kind of sense in this re-telling, as though the narrator has run out of patience with the neediness, the vulnerability, the incessant dithering of Jesus' disciples . . . has run out of patience, and decided that it is high time the baby church relinquish its absorption with what used to be, and get on with making a new creation. In Acts, Jesus does not merely "teach," he does not "open their minds," he does not "bless," not at all: rather, he *instructs,* he *orders,* he rebukes them for their endless, pointless questions, and then, as if in a huff, he is taken up, and disappears. This time around, Luke does not bother to suggest that the disciples were filled with joy, or that they went anywhere *worshipping*—anything but! These disciples, abandoned literally in mid-sentence, stand right where they are, rooted to the ground, eyes fixed on the heavens and mouths agape—as if freezing the frame of the picture will somehow make everything all better.

What makes these two stories so different?

On Friday night, Aimee's mom and step-dad and I threw a party to celebrate her graduation from college. We invited her siblings and step-siblings, her grandparents and parents, her friends and teachers to join us in remembering Aimee's past with stories and pictures and mementos of the child who was. We played music, told stories, showed pictures, reminded her of who she was, and who each of us once had been in her life. We watched a video, put together from grainy old eight millimeter home movies, showing Aimee the baby, the toddler, the child, the actress. Throughout the evening, that group of relatives and former relatives who, truth to tell, do not usually get along all that well, exclaimed at our common ground—*oh, I remember that couch. Why, we have that couch now. Look, there's Danny! And Nonnie! Oh, the donkey song! we used to dance, remember?* In a few magical minutes, the unconnected and broken strands of the past came together as we made common cause, connected

---

12. Acts 1:7, RSV.

with our history and wove around Aimee a mighty tapestry of memory. The evening was a gift, and not just, I think, for Aimee.

I read again Luke's twenty-fourth chapter, the first Ascension story, and I think: the apostle realized that remembering is an important part of moving on. Looking back at who we were, at the old stories of our lives and our ancestors and our faith—this isn't mere sentimentality, nostalgia for a vanished way of believing and knowing the world, but a powerful evoking of what used to be, in the service of what is to come. A child needs a past to face the future. A family, even one broken by divorce and death, needs to remember the ties that knitted them together once in joy, if they are to make new beginnings flow gently out of the deep waters of what used to be. And yet, we are casual with our history, sometimes, even scornful of it. Sacred or common, we have grown fond of examining the stories of our heritage, and discarding them without a second glance—*couldn't have happened,* we say about some tale in the Bible, *it's myth. It reflects an antiquated worldview,* we say, and of course it does, though why that should stop us from remembering, I cannot imagine. We have learned to scrutinize the old pictures, the buried tales, the forgotten verses of our faith and of our lives with surprise and a certain sense of reticence: *I don't remember that,* we say—or, more painfully, *I don't want to remember* that.

But Luke wants us to remember—he knows how important it is that we do remember: and so Jesus, before he leaves his disciples behind, tells stories. Reads the Scriptures. Points out the connections. Reminds them. Weaves about them a shimmering web of memory and power and nostalgia and love, so that when he is gone, and they are on their own, they will know in the midst of absence, where they come from, who they are, and how they have been, and always will be, beloved.

Remembering is important, but it is not enough. On Friday night, in the midst of nostalgia and celebration, there were bunches of balloons and festively wrapped gifts—*congratulations, graduate!* but floating above them, a prophetic utterance, inscribed on a brightly glowing blue star, and it said: *Get a job.* There are times to remember, and times to move on. No parent wants to evoke in a grown child nostalgia for the past so powerful that the graduate wants nothing more than to come home and have mommy take care of him again. No older adult, facing a change in the season of life due to the death of a spouse, or the anticipating of infirmity, wants to spend so much time reflecting on what *was* that they become captivated by memory, crippled by the past, wholly unable to take the necessary next step into a new stage of life with courage and with hope. We need more than the past to fit us for the future, else we stay fixed and fixated—like the disciples in Act's first chapter, standing with mouths open on an unanswered question as Jesus disappears from their midst, wholly unready to relinquish what used to be or to consider what might, happily come next in their lives. There are some times when memory must be set aside in order that the future can have a place in our lives to take root and grow. Times when we need something more to help us to move on.

At the opening of the book of Acts, Luke needs to tell the disciples' story in a different way. The time for memory is past. The time for grieving is gone. The need to comfort, to recall, to celebrate, to look backward, is over. Now, there is a job to do. A church to grow. A group of people who have been trained and fitted for their new work in the world . . . but who do not yet quite believe that they are ready. Now, before the bickering begins over what to pack and what to leave behind, before the arguing commences about who is an adult and who's making the decisions about how late to stay out and when to hit the road, now, before the uncertainty and the fear of what may be on the horizon entirely paralyzes the future, *now* it is time to tell the story in a different way.

And so Luke does: he shows them how unflattering it is, to be a disciple locked in the past, a child who will not grow up, an older person who cannot let go of the past, a broken family consumed with bitterness and recrimination and grief. He shows them as they are, or as they could become: mouths agape, fists extended, breath caught on a final, frozen, *No!* and he says: *it doesn't have to be like this.*

The past is a tool, not a prison. You are ready to move on. What you had before, will never leave you entirely. You are ready to move on. You believe you are alone, but there are angels beside you, pointing the way. You are ready to move on.

You are uncertain, and more than a little afraid, but look, *you will receive power when the Holy Spirit comes upon you, and you will be my witnesses.*[13] You are ready to move on. It is ascension, the Holy Spirit is just around the corner: *God has gone up with a merry shout,* and so should we, for by the grace of God, braced by memory and blessed with power, we are ready to move on.

---

13. Acts 1:8, NRSV.

The Acts of Orchids

ASCENSION: ACTS 1

(in memory of Norman)

Eyes dry
Faces set against the merciless glare
We stared into the sun
      the careful rules forgotten
            until we were certain

—Dead sure—
that god was gone for good.

It was something we had,
      unfortunately,
           long suspected.
Standing in the empty heat
side by side, and yet alone
It seemed a blessing, almost: When
the cloud that shrouded the sun
obscured our view of you
      eclipsed as well our last image of
          a hand raised in Warning
              Blessing?
Or maybe just to say good-bye.

It was time to go home.
Under the mercy of the Cloud
      our hearts, less clear
turned back to smaller things:
         a bird
         a voice
         a song, a prayer

Our hearts, as I said, less fear
skipped a beat
lifted with the sudden breeze—
      the Spirit-wind that blew
           stinging our eyes with unexpected moisture

Or,
quite possibly,
with healing tears.

6

The Greening of the Gospel

The Festival of Pentecost Through Christ the King

I LOVE PENTECOST, THE last major church holy day not to have been co-opted by secular sensibilities and interests. No trees, gifts, bunnies, eggs, or Santas intrude on my pure enjoyment of the festival most of us mark as the birthday of the Church as told in the second chapter of the book of Acts. Through the years, it is become a big deal in the congregation I serve: we do it up right, with balloons, cantatas, special music, instruments, food, noise, and color, and the voices of many languages. Curiously, though, as we have celebrated through the years, I have come to learn that it is not the high holiday aspect of Pentecost that engages my spirit . . . but instead, the way in which our celebration of that event calls to attention the small gifts and graces, the little stories and idiosyncrasies of the people who make up the church of Jesus Christ in this place. It is just like the story said, *they were all together in one place. Tongues as of fire appeared among them, and rested on each of them. And they all were filled with the Holy Spirit and began to speak . . .*[1] Pentecost is a time in our congregation for people, children and adults alike, who customarily do not speak out in public to tell their faith stories: a Cuban immigrant tells a story of learning to be at home in her adopted country. A survivor of World War II internment camps speaks softly about overcoming prejudice against the Japanese . . . because of the command of Jesus Christ to welcome the stranger. A gay man describes his homecoming to God, within the community of our congregation. A Sunday school teacher gives thanks for the gift of his students. Children sing. People write prayers in languages they learned from a grandfather, a mother, a friend, in a homeland far across

1. Acts 2:1–4.

the ocean—and the prayers of the people become a joyful cacophony of familiar voices speaking strange words, one on top of the other. At the conclusion, when the Lord's prayer draws us back together, red balloons, tied with prayers, are released to ascend to a ceiling where they bump and whisper together, forming a long, red line at the peak of the sanctuary roof, the blood ties of our people. Pentecost is over, and the church begins again.

One Pentecost Sunday, the sacrament of the Lord's Supper followed the prayers. As is our custom, groups of congregants gathered in circles around the communion table to share the meal and offer their gifts to God. As they prayed and passed the bread and wine around, a rogue balloon floated down from the ceiling, up the aisle and into the communion circle. Around the table it floated, as if seeking something, or someone. It came to a stop at shoulder level just in front of the bowed figure of one of our older women, a Greek immigrant beloved to all of us. Every year, Fofo would offer to read a prayer in her native Greek language . . . and then, at the last moment, as church began, tell me that it was too much, she could not handle the strain of public recitation. She was often anxious, and frequently prone to drama. In the communion circle, she prayed silently, earnestly—probably, after all, in Greek. The balloon hovered. People smiled, and waited. Finally, Fofo looked up, jumped, and batted the balloon over toward the communion table. *Ach! Po, po, po,* she wailed, tapping her breast and shaking her head, and the room erupted in warm, loving laughter. It took only a moment for Fofo also to begin to grin and to celebrate—her special moment as the center of the Pentecost festivities.

Ordinary Time—those long weeks that follow Pentecost, leading us through the hot days of summer and the languid waning heat of fall, move me in just the same way. It is as if a breath from the Spirit has floated down from the ceiling, from the heights of celebration, just to rest on the small lives and the ordinary stories of the people of God, both in life and in the Bible. It hovers before first one unsuspecting soul, and then another. It takes its time, and chooses well. We have time—weeks and weeks and weeks of it—to slow down, take a second look, and lavish attention on people, events, and places that are often overlooked or given short shrift during the church's headlong rush through the story of Jesus' life as it has been encapsulated between Advent and Easter.

In ordinary time, we are afforded long, slow walks through the in-the-beginnings of Genesis. We get to know Abraham and Hagar and Sarah, their terrible family dynamics and their staggering faith in God.

We pour over the Jacob cycle, with its summer beach reading pot-boiler-like twists and turns. We get past the Sunday school picture of King David, the shepherd boy who became king, and learn what it is like to struggle for the grace of God through a flawed life filled with passion and power and prayer. We walk along with the Hebrew children, their long, weary way through the wilderness toward a land of promise, and we ponder our own ways. Lingering over the parables and healing stories of Jesus as over dessert, we are able to savor their flavor and appreciate them for what they are, not merely for their place in the great drama of salvation. We think about our own lives, our own stories, and how they mingle and entwine with the old, old story. We mark where we were last year, and dream about what we might yet become.

There are over a score of Sundays in this long, green season, wholly half the church year: time enough to enjoy the indulgence of rocking on the porch on a warm starlit night, listening to the soft voices of elders, talking about old times and how they have shaped the life that is the gift of *now*. These are my favorite weeks, this ordinary time, and when Advent rushes up with its passionate urgency to begin again, its klaxon warnings of judgment, and its sweet call to *repent, for the kingdom of heaven is at hand*, I am almost sorry to see it come to an end.

Ordinary time is a season for paying slow, sweet attention to the everyday. For delving deep, when so often we merely skim the surface, so anxious are we to get to the point. A friend of mine, a busy pastor of several rural small churches in the Bahamas, was notified by his part time secretary that a parishioner had died, and she needed information to prepare the service. *Ok,* he said, *I can't get over to you this afternoon, but I'll tell you what. The service for Mary Johnson is still on my computer—I'll do something of the same thing for Edna. Just hit the "add/change" function on the word processor to change "Mary" to "Edna," and I'll pick it up right before the service.* And he did, and proceeded through the service until the congregation rose to its feet at the close of worship and recited together their affirmation of faith: *I believe in God the Father almighty maker of heaven and earth and in Jesus Christ his only son our Lord who was conceived by the Holy Ghost, born of the virgin Edna . . .*

Living on automatic may be a great time saver, but if we do not take care, the greening of the gospel may be happening all the time, all around us, and we will not see it. *God is in the details,* Schweitzer said once, and the gift of ordinary time is the chance to look, and taste, and see.

The Greening of the Gospel

PENTECOST SUNDAY

Genesis 11:1-9   John 20:19-23   Acts 2:1-21

Once Upon a Time...

Once upon a time

> isn't that how all stories begin?
> Stories told to soothe children before they sleep
> Stories told to scare the disobedient—
> Stories told to teach and to inspire—
> They all begin the same.

Once upon a time—

> This one is an old, old story.
> So old, the reason it was originally written has been lost,
> > as lost as the city whose tale it tells,
>
> Crumbled into ruins and dust.
> The reasons and the city are lost, but the story remains—
> And for our own purposes, we tell it again and again.

Once upon a time, there was a city.

> It was a great city, a populous city. A river city. A dangerous city.
> This city was so dangerous that at night, the authorities would remove
> > all the boards from the only bridge over the river—
>
> So that people from either half of the city would be prevented
> > from robbing each other blind.[2]

I guess, by our standards, it was a pretty typical city.

But to the people who told this story, the city of Babylon
  —or *Babel,* as the ancient Jews called it—
  was anything but typical.
It was the greatest city in the history of the world.
The cradle of civilization.
It was a cesspool of evil, a godless wasteland.

---

2. Brueggemann, *Interpreter's Dictionary of the Bible*, vol. 1, 334f.

Tuning My Heart

When, much later, the Jews were forced to go there, they sang:

> *By the waters of Babylon,*
> > *there we sat down and wept,*
> > > *when we remembered Zion. (Psalm 137)*
> I guess it depended upon who you were asking.
> And when.

But on this long ago, hot summer's day,
> By anyone's standards
> Babel was a great city.
> Ten thousand Babylonians were hard at work,
> > toiling in the relentless sun.
> The breeze that blew over the city that day
> > gave little relief
> > and smelled of fish and mud.
> Still, when it rattled the dry grasses,
> > And swept the dust into whirling funnels,
> Ten thousand hot, sweaty Babylonians
> > lifted up their faces to the breeze
> > and sighed.

It was time for a rest.

But about that time, the Lord God Almighty came down.
> Came strolling into town like a tourist on holiday.
> Just to see—
> > To see the legendary city.
> To see what ten thousand laboring Babylonians were up to.

> And when God saw it,
> > When God saw the tower they were building
> > > That had looked so small from the heights of heaven
> > > > But so big now from the ground,
> > When God saw it—
> > It was beautiful
> > But it was not good.

The people of Babylon were, the Lord God discovered,
> Afraid.

The Greening of the Gospel

They were afraid of being scattered—
    of losing who they were, and what they had.
They had been nomads once,
    but now they had found a home.
    They were determined never ever to be scattered again.
    and they founded a city.
They were determined to make a name for themselves.
    And they had.
    They had done all that—

And they were not scattered.
    They were one.   United.

But it was not a *one-nation-under-god* sort of unity
    No, it had very little to do with God.

Rather, the people of Babylon were united
    Like racial purists are united,
bent on ethnic cleansing
or segregation
    Like schoolchildren are united
        against the ugly duckling newcomer
    Like a neighborhood is united
        against a homeless shelter on the air force base or
        against low income houses being built
            And scattered throughout their so-called
            "community"
The people of Babylon were united, all right,
    and besides that,
        they had one language.

    A language so well understood,
        so universal
    That they needed only a few, choice words.

Words like: *you are not welcome here.*
    Go to hell.

The people of Babylon were one people—
    One like a nation united for nothing except its own well-being.

Tuning My Heart

One like a corporation committed to nothing but profit
One like a church, united for no purpose except its own comfort.

The people of Babylon were one people, with one language
    And they needed only a few words, like:
    Mine.

They were, as one scholar has said,
    a fearful humanity organized against the purposes of God.[3]
And God was having none of it.

So the Lord God Almighty came down to the city
    and blew through town
    and when all was said and done

The tower was empty.
The people were gone,
    their languages confounded
    their unity broken
        scattered, just as they had feared.

    And a great evil was prevented that day.

We tell that story to explain why there are so many different languages
    And why the peoples of the earth
        just can't work together.

Once upon a time—
    Now, this is another old story—

Once upon a time, there was another city
    a city under occupation.
    A city that was far from lawless.

    In fact, just that weekend
        during a major religious festival
        three criminals had been executed by crucifixion,
            high up on a hill in the center of town.
        Upholding the law.

---

3. Brueggemann, Walter, *Interpretation: A Bible Commentary for Teaching and Preaching; Genesis,* 100.

The Greening of the Gospel

    That city was called Jerusalem.

    People were stunned.
        And some people were afraid.
        The breeze blowing through the city that day
            was not so hot—
                in fact, it was quite pleasant.
        But the eleven men locked in a stuffy second story room
            On a not-so-nice-street
              in an out-of-the-way corner of Jerusalem
                did not feel the breeze.

They had locked the doors,
        and sealed all the windows
    For fear.

And that is what the Lord God found
    while strolling into town that afternoon
    together with the son with whom he had been recently reunited.
The Lord God went to visit his friends,
    but found them afraid
        grief-stricken
        locked up.

And beholding that fear, God saw that it was a terrible sight,
    a terrible thing to be locked up in broad daylight.

    Like Haitian children,
locked in a hotel room while their mother fights for asylum
Like children in our neighborhoods who are not allowed outside to
    play,
        lest they catch a stray bullet…
Like churches that want everything to be the way it was
in the good old days.

God saw their fear,
    as I was saying,
        And God knew that it was not good.

Tuning My Heart

The men had been there for over a week
>and the room was very stuffy, reeking with fear
>>and heavy with regret
>when the Lord God's holy son walked through the locked door
>>and sat down to dinner with his friends.

Peace be with you, he said.
And he showed them his hands and side, and how,
>though they had put him to death,
>>mere death could not hold him,
>And he was free.[4]

Receive the holy spirit, he said.
And he breathed on them.
>And the touch of his breath was like a gentle springtime breeze
>>in Jerusalem ... fragrant and refreshing.

It was the same fresh air that was,
>even then,
>>blowing through the city of Jerusalem ...

Except they could not feel it
>because they were still locked up inside.

Jesus had given them peace, but they didn't know what to do with it.

And that could have been the end of the story
>>Which would have made it, I guess,
>A sad story, told to inspire ...
>>but somehow not quite pulling it off.

But by God, it was *not* the end of the story.

Once upon a time—
>again in Jerusalem, not long after the last story
>>but long enough.
>Long enough for Jesus to have gone away again—this time for good.
>Long enough for the disciples to wonder

---

4. John 20.

The Greening of the Gospel

What now?
How shall we live?
What would he want us to do?

Not long,
    only about fifty days
        but long enough for those disciples in the upper room
            to have learned how to pray.

Once upon a time,
    It was festival time in Jerusalem again.

This one was called Pentecost.
    Like Mardi Gras in Rio
        or New Orleans
    It drew thousands of visitors
        Foreigners,
    From all over the world.

From everywhere, friends and enemies alike gathered in Jerusalem that day.
    The babble of languages was astounding.
        Deafening.
        Overwhelming.
It was the city of Babylon all over again.
    Except that no one could understand anyone else.

    But it probably didn't matter to the tourists:
        They were there for the party.

And so was the Lord God Almighty,
    just like before,
        like so many befores—
    The Lord God Almighty came strolling into town on the day of Pentecost
        to visit and redeem the people.

There was a lot to see, and even more to hear . . .

> And the music of the voices God heard was beautiful in its diversity
>> but the words they spoke were not very good.

God heard Palestinians and Israelis arguing over who owned the holy land.
God heard Americans arguing with Mexicans
> and removing the boards from the bridges
>> so that no one else could come in,
and the homeland could be secure.
God heard people threatening to leave the Church if
> "those kind of people" were allowed to worship, and pray,
>> and serve, and lead just like everyone else.

God didn't much like what God was hearing
> And there were too many words and no understanding.
> It seemed like God was the only one listening…
But one thing God did *not* hear,
> one thing, for which God had been listening
>> very closely…

> Where, in the midst of all that cacophony,
>> were the voices of the Way?

> Where were the voices charged with the peace of Jesus?
>> Where were the men and women who had been
>>> given the power
>>>> to lock or unlock
>>> the gates of the new Jerusalem,
>>> the kin-dom of heaven?[5]

Where in the world were they?
God listened,
> And God walked very carefully through the streets of the city,
>> listening at doors
>>> and peering through windows
> And finally, God found what he was looking for.

---

5. I am indebted to theologian Ada Maria Isasi-Diaz for the image of the reign of God expressed in the term "kin-dom."

The Greening of the Gospel

Those disciples, God's friends
    still in the upper room
    still afraid.
        Praying, at least
            but not doing much else.

And though there was no wind in the city that day,
    or so the story goes

    The Lord God blew through town—
        And was mightily exercised
            and altogether worked up
        over the voices of the strangers squabbling in the streets
        and the silence of the praying disciples in their locked
            room.

And the Lord God Almighty blew through that house.
    And the walls shook with the power of it.
        It was like a tornado, a hurricane
            It was like nothing they could have imagined.

And after the wind, there was fire:
        And just like the Lord God had come down,
    so the fire went up that day—
        divided tongues,
            resting on each of them.
        No one was spared,
    And no one was scattered.

They were all together in one place,
    shaking with the wind,
        and tingling with the power of the fire.

And then, at last, they spoke as God had hoped.
    They spoke: and again,
        It was like Babel, reversed.
    It was not one language, but many
        And the reasons were not evil, but good.

Tuning My Heart

They all spoke the amazing deeds of God in many tongues,
    And what is more, they all heard,
    Each in their own language.

And all over that city, the squabbling stopped.
    And the people ran to the little house to see.
    And they saw, and they heard—

And what they heard was Love
And what they saw was the spirit of Jesus blowing through those
    Tired, frightened men and women—

And making a new thing.
    A new language.
        And for once, they all understood.
    And the disciples learned why what Jesus had breathed on them
        was Peace.

And they were no longer scattered.
    And they were set free.
        And that was the birth-day of the church.

Once upon a time—
    It was a hot summer day in Miami, Florida—
        and the breeze which blew off the ocean
            smelled of jacaranda
            and of salt,
                and a little bit, of mud.

    And some of the people were in church.
        The doors were not locked,
            but the air conditioners were going
        So the people could not always hear
            The sounds of the city outside
                Or feel the breezes.
        But they were not afraid.
            And they knew the stories.

The Greening of the Gospel

And when the Lord God Almighty came walking down Sunset Drive
    they opened up the doors,
and went out into the light
    And it was Pentecost.
    Again.

ORDINARY TIME

(Sunday after the Fourth of July)

Genesis 24

E Pluribus Unum

I remember the last Independence Day that I felt like an American in church. I was in the middle of seminary, and had traveled to upstate New York to visit my husband who was serving a summer chaplaincy at Rome Air Force Base. I drove north with a mounting sense of excitement—Independence Day on base—the closest I had come to being "home" in a very long time. On Sunday, we attended Protestant Chapel. I glanced down at the bulletin—yes, all my favorite hymns were there. I was suffused with a sense of familiar peace—the chaplains in uniform, the young servicemen in the back, the clean-cut looking families, even the barren architecture of the chapel felt like home to me. The trumpet fanfare of the opening hymn exploded from the organ: *God of our Fathers, whose almighty hand* . . . I sang with gusto, as did every other soul in the room with the exception of two Korean women, sitting in the pew in front of me. The service went on—the scriptures, the sermon, a stirring call to the highest and best patriotism a people of faith could offer their country. *My Country, Tis of Thee* was next: almost a prayer, I thought, tears filling my eyes as I sang; noticing that, once again, the Korean women were silent in the pew ahead. I settled back in my seat, vaguely troubled. Why were they not singing? Did they not know the hymns? Was it possible they did not speak English? They seemed to be participating in the prayers and other liturgy. . . . The third hymn rang out—*O Beautiful, for Spacious Skies*—one of my favorites, but my voice fell silent less than halfway through the first verse as I watched the silent Koreans and finally got it: how could they sing the Lord's song in a strange land? Or, more accurately—how could they sing a strange land's song in the Lord's house? They were aliens, not Americans, they did not belong; and as the service of worship wore on I felt my sense of belonging and comfort and peace drain away, leaving me empty and silent, like the women in the pew before me, strangers in a strange land.

No matter who we are, no matter where we come from, we all belong somewhere—somewhere makes our heart swell with pride—or with yearning. Some faces look like us, and others do not Some of us see a skinny, sunburned *balsero,* struggling ashore on a beach in Surfside, and our hearts are wrung with pity, our energy stirred, our bodies moving with haste to block the highways and bridges of our adopted land to show our solidarity with our people, our kind.

Some of us, stuck on the Palmetto Expressway, perhaps, or watching from home, study the waving Cuban flags and the hordes of angry immigrants shouting *libertad!* with a sense of confusion, or even anger. We love our people, too, and the secret, politically incorrect heart murmurs, *if they love Cuba so much, why don't they go home?*

We all belong somewhere, somewhere is home to us, or should be: Northern Ireland, Protestant England, the Palestinian West Bank, Jerusalem the golden, Croatia, Serbia, Bosnia-Herzegovina, Darfur, Burma, Myanmar.

We all belong somewhere; I talked to my daughter once, away on the beach with her dad's wife's family. Her voice was small and far-away, and she sounded like a little girl as she said, *mommy, I want to come home. These people are not of my blood.*

We all belong somewhere; and in our belonging, we fall prey to a potent mixture of pride, patriotism, preference, and prejudice that can, on the one hand, empower us to great accomplishments . . . but on the other, may cripple us with competing claims of loyalty, and a vision too easily circumscribed by faces and accents and landscapes like us—that cause others to slip away into a threatening, alien *them,* a people not of our blood.

We all belong somewhere, and this where Abraham's dilemma begins, near the end of his long and fruitful life, as he contemplates the future of generations in the person of his marriage-aged son. Abraham is an heir of the promise, and he loves his new land, but he hates the people—the Canaanites—who are his neighbors in it. Abraham loves his blood, but views his ancestral home, Haran, as a barren land, a place where the future is closed and dead. Between the blood that he loves and the new land to which he has been called stands Isaac, his son: a boy in whom the seed of the future lies waiting. Where does Isaac belong? And with whom?

The Greening of the Gospel

Calling his oldest, most trusted servant, Abraham charges him with the reconciliation of the future. *Swear you will not get a wife for my son from the daughters of the Canaanites, among whom I live, but will go to my country and my kindred and get a wife for my son Isaac.*[6] In his voice, there is a dripping venom for those people—those neighbors whose ways he does not understand, and whose practices are revolting to him. In his eyes, as he charges his servant, is a world of anxiety and conviction: his son must remain with his own kind, must marry one of "us." And the servant, getting it, probes further into his responsibilities to Abraham's blood: *And if she will not come?* inquires the servant, innocently, *should I then take Isaac home?* But the answer comes with a resistance and conviction as strong as his aversion to the people of Canaan: *No! Whatever you do, see to it that you do not take my son back there.*[7]

Hearing him, we are with Abraham: looking at our own children, we identify with his hopes, his fears, his sense of being torn between divided loyalties, his prejudice and his straining toward the future. We want our children to belong, we want our heritage to remain secure, we want—

But wait. This is not about what we want, not about what Abraham wants. For Abraham's story is over, and now the world must go on, with Isaac and his unknown bride as the bridge to the future, the future of which Abraham dreamed and in which God promised: *You will be blessed to be a blessing, and in you all the families of the earth will be blessed.* So this story is not about what was, but rather, about what is to come. It is not about Abraham, but about the one who bridges the vast gap between the bound, limited, torn present and the open expansive future—the future in which this parochial, suspicious patriarch's clan can at last become what it was meant to be: a family in which *all* of the families of the earth could be blessed.

And who is this one? It is not Isaac, passive recipient of a father's prejudice and a future's promise. Nor is it Rebekah, daughter of adventure, willing though she is to place her life in the hands of promise. It is not her brother Laban, captivated by his blood and shaped by his responsibilities to the ancestral household. None of these holds the future of the people of God, but one does:

---

6. Genesis 24:3–4, NRSV.
7. Genesis 24:6, NRSV.

And that one is a nameless, faceless servant—motivated by love, enriched by the past, made bold by a vision of the future lodged in the subtle, homely movements of the spirit of God, who will somehow draw a man and a woman together in love, and create a bridge of possibility into the future.

This is his story, and as he tells it, we learn how ordinary, invisible people—people just like us, bound by their heritage and torn among competing claims on our loyalty—can open ourselves up to the journey, and make a home for the hopes of the kingdom of God. Going on his way, he watches, he thinks, he looks carefully at the faces of strangers, he prays, he believes; God will show him in the faces of strangers, the possibility of kin, and the way home. Believing, he places himself at the disposal of the universe, and listens for the voice whose Spirit causes chance encounters to resonate with purpose and power; and whose call makes kinfolk out of strangers.

And we learn; generally, it is not the powerful and the named who build the bridges that carry us from the old lands of suspicion and isolation and fragmentation into the new country of trust and community. It is the invisible, the unnamed, the servants—the people we have forgotten, who carry the future for us, for all of us. And sometimes, by the grace of God, it is even us, the people of God rising above our clannishness and our lack of understanding of whatever group of people does not look like us or act like us or speak English—or Spanish—like we do. Sometimes, we are the servants—the unknown and unregarded ones who see beyond the failures of national boundaries and doctrine and creed to the heart of the promise beneath. We try to laugh when we are cut off in traffic by someone who learned how to drive on another planet, or stand in an elevator in our own home town with people speaking a language we barely understand. We laugh and work to remain open and easy with the threatening strangeness of it all, because we know our world is, should be, bigger than only that which makes us comfortable.

We labor to pass a living wage, for *justice for all*. We witness and work to keep a human rights ordinance alive in Miami because *we hold these truths to be self-evident, that all people are created equal*. We see power *still* in promises that have been broken, by others and by us, more times than we can number. We see *still* the unbreakable thread of the fidelity of God weaving itself through the tangles, the knots, and the frayed ends of the tapestry of promise that is for all of us, not just for some. And we know *we* bear the responsibility, the possibility, and the freedom to make the connections, to find the bridge to the future, to believe after all that the promises of God are faithful. For we are the people of God, coming again and again to the table where *they shall come from north and south and from east and west to sit in the kingdom of God,* nameless servants who take up our work to build the invisible, fragile bridges between the lands whose allegiance claims us and the far country toward which the promise of God calls us—home. Amen.

ORDINARY TIME

2 Samuel 11:1–15

Homemade Sin

Hearing this morning's Scripture, you might think you were reading a transcript of the Jerry Springer show, rather than listening for the word of God. There is just nothing uplifting, holy, or, well, *biblical* about this tale of the sordid fall of Israel's golden boy, King David, who used his power to serve his lust, who took what he wanted without pity, and who, in serving his own transitory need, shattered the lives of an innocent woman and her soldier husband, setting his own family's fortunes on a downward spiral toward destruction.

Church folk read the Bible to be inspired, not disgusted—we want to elevate our lives. We come to church for better, not for worse—and if any of our own personal histories bear the burden of some similar story of shame—well, that is not for church, but instead is a secret best kept hidden, even from ourselves.

I had a professor of pastoral counseling in seminary who made this fact abundantly clear while teaching us how to minister to parishioners in crisis. Before she brought into class some "real" people whose personal and familial problems were to be addressed by us in counseling, she would introduce their issues—adultery, alcoholism, financial misfeasance, abuse—and with a grimace of distaste on her face and a shake of her head would conclude *this situation is as ugly as homemade sin.* From which I learned that, at church and in the family of God, some folks' troubles were just too nasty to talk about; too ugly to be redeemed.

But this morning, just for a few minutes, the Bible—the Bible—would ask us to believe that even homemade sin is not too ugly to be unveiled, too awful to examine, too far beyond redemption to be offered up to God and to God's people. This morning, the Bible offers us a rare opportunity to listen to one such story—a story as ugly as homemade sin—and to find in it, a word from God.

This is a story that, as scholar Walter Brueggemann puts it, reveals *more than we want to know about David and more than we can bear to understand about ourselves.* It is a story that cuts deep into *the strange web of foolishness, fear, and fidelity that comprises the human map.*[8]

This is a story about David—or maybe about any one of us, a story about what happens when a person experiences a failure of vocation, a loss of meaning, a breakdown of identity, a surge of ruthlessness or recklessness that, once indulged, changes the landscape of family, faith, and life forever. It is a story about a seventeen-year-old girl in Pinecrest, Florida, a little tipsy, who smashed her car into a tree and ended another girl's life. It is a story about the john on the street, the neighbor whom desperation led to "borrow" money from his company's coffers but who was caught before he could repay it. It is a story about a husband, a wife, a stranger whom you would never have suspected . . . it is a story about you, or about me.

In the spring of the year, when kings go forth to battle, David stayed home.[9] His place was with his soldiers in the field, but his heart, lulled by security, had turned in boredom to matters of power, and of lust. How strange, that stories of human tragedy can be told so pitilessly, with such brevity and baldness. It happened. He saw a woman. He sent. He lay with her. She conceived. She told him, "I am pregnant." Told so coldly, what are we to believe? How are we to feel? Where are the explanations, the details, the mitigating circumstances? Where is the personal charm that will permit us to understand, to excuse, to embrace David and what he has done with compassion and grace? How are we to feel, when nothing and no one is spared in the telling of this old and ugly story?

Like David, our first reaction is to deny, to cover up, to hide. We are not that kind of person. He would never do anything like that. Maybe she will never find out. There must be some reasonable explanation. Maybe if I get busy, have a drink, get a lawyer, start over again somewhere else, strike a bargain, pretend a lot and lie a little, this mistake can be erased as if it never existed, and I can have my life back again, the way it was before.

---

8 Brueggemann, *Interpretation: A Bible Commentary for Teaching and Preaching; 1 and 2 Samuel*, 272.

9. 2 Samuel 11:1, NRSV.

We listen to David, and we watch him, trying to repair the shattered fragments of his life and Bathsheba's, and sadness fills us. Calling the man he has betrayed in from the field of battle, David seeks for peace, yearns for it like a man dying of thirst in a desert of his own creation. *Is it well with Joab? With the war? With you? With the people? Is everything okay?* Uriah does not know, but David does, that nothing is okay—not now, and perhaps not ever again—and no assurance of peace, offered in ignorance of the truth, can touch this pain David carries. For David alone knows what he is: he bears the pain of his fall from grace in secrecy and shame. He believes that the love of God cannot reach him there: and so believing, he despairs and compounds the wreckage he has made of his life by committing murder. The secret must be kept for David to survive; and so, Uriah must die—and with him, the last of the shining innocence of the shepherd boy who became king, and the last of that man's hope and trust in the saving power of Love.

In short order, the story rushes to its unhappy conclusion. Uriah returns. Joab obeys. The soldier dies, and a messenger is sent with the news to David, who now must pay the additional cost of the hardening of his soul against his comrades, his people, his friends. *People die,* he shrugs, swallowing against the grief. *It is the way of battle. Do not be troubled*, he tells the messenger to tell Joab, and it is evident that it is himself he is trying to convince. And the story tells us: *the thing was not evil in David's eyes.* And how could it be? For deadening the conscience to the soul's cry of pain is the only way David can now survive in the script he is penning for his life.

Or is it?

Could it be . . . that there is something bigger at work in David and in Israel than power, and cynicism and fear? Something that will not abide a cover up that deadens the soul of a man and cripples the future of a family, a people, and a land? Something that will not let sleeping dogs lie; something that is standing for the possibility of truth when silence might have been enough to get by?

The narrator of this story knows what that Something is, and he names it: *Now the thing was evil in the eyes of the Lord.*[10] "The thing" was good enough for the broken David; but it was not good enough for David's God. And so God's people found the courage to tell this story, and to tell it straight—as ugly and impossible as it was.

---

10. 2 Samuel 11:27, RSV.

Where before in David's life there were circumstances, explanations, justifications—just like in our own lives—where before, there were reasons to explain away the truth, to distance the knowing of self, to silence the voice of God; now, there is inexplicably a new power at work.

A people willing to open their eyes and face the truth about the golden boy of Israel. A family willing to share the cost of David's mistakes. A genuine possibility that a man might be loved, not despite, but in the midst of, his brokenness and his flaws. An astounding, ground-breaking, reckless new trust in truth—and in truth's God—that calls the people to tell it like it is, let the chips fall where they may, and listen for a saving, a judging, a healing word from God.

This story has guts. It asks us: does faith mean perfection, or does it mean trust, even in the midst of brokenness? It asks us: is fidelity about the appearance of goodness? Or about a willingness to persist and to begin again to live for the Good, even in the midst of shattering, ego-breaking failure and sin?

It tells us something very important about the nature of God and about the possibilities of a life sustained by God's grace: that God works for good even in, or perhaps especially in, the deeply flawed and terrible circumstances of lives broken by sin and hidden in the lie. The old hymn says it as well as anything else:

> *There's a wideness in God's mercy like the wideness of the sea*
> *There's a kindness in God's justice which is more than liberty.*
> *There is no place where earth's sorrows are more felt than up in heaven.*
> *There is no place where earth's failings have such kindly judgment given.*[11]

ORDINARY TIME

Mark 9:38–50   *Esther (selections)*

"More Immediate Concerns"

Since this morning our Jewish neighbors celebrate *Rosh Hashanah*, the beginning of the New Year, it is perhaps felicitous that the *Christian*

---

11. *There's a Wideness in God's Mercy,* The Hymnbook, Presbyterian Church USA, Philadelphia: 1945, No. 110.

The Greening of the Gospel

Revised Common Lectionary has served up for our consideration the story of Queen Esther. Buried in the middle of the wisdom literature in the Hebrew Scriptures, and only presented for Christian consideration on this *one* Sunday out of three full years of appointed readings; it tells a story that provides the backdrop for the Jewish midwinter festival of Purim. This melodrama in ten short chapters tells the tale of the deliverance of Jewish exiles in Persia from extermination at the hands of a powerful enemy, Haman, thanks to the wisdom of the old man Mordecai and the wily, devious courage of the beautiful Queen Esther.

Here is the story, told in brief: Esther, a virgin Jewess, wins a contest and joins the harem of King Ahasuerus, whose main talent seems to be for partying. Her uncle Mordecai cautions her to hide her religious identity, and, doing the same himself, becomes one of the king's trusted advisors. His colleague, the evil Haman, has an overweening ego and malice to spare. He tricks the king into passing a law that will result in the extermination of all Jews in the kingdom. Mordecai, grief-stricken and hysterical, appeals to the girl Esther: *if you keep silence at such a time as this, relief and deliverance will rise for the people from another quarter, but you and your father's family will perish. Who knows? Perhaps you have come to royal dignity for just such a time as this.*[12] Though Esther risks her life if she comes uninvited into the king's presence, she nevertheless devises a plan, relying heavily on intrigue, the king's lust and drunkenness, and her own sexuality to expose Haman and save her people. When all is said and done, Esther's cleverness and adaptability to circumstance and necessity have won the day, and the feast of Purim is instituted as a perpetual memorial to the power of the downtrodden when pushed to the wall: (that day) *had been turned for them from sorrow into gladness and from mourning into a holiday; that they should make them days of feasting and gladness, days for sending gifts of food to one another and presents to the poor.*[13]

Purim is not your granny's church holy day. It is, like the story that spawned it, a boisterous celebration, replete with eating, drinking, and playful, outrageous behavior. Many synagogues observe Purim with a carnival: children and adults alike dress up in costumes, and frequently the "megillah" of Esther is acted out as well as read, with enthusiastic audience partici-

---

12. Esther 4:14, NRSV.
13. Esther 9:22, NRSV.

pation—it is the *Rocky Horror Picture Show* of Scripture, a place where the Bible and vaudeville share the stage, and everybody gets involved.

Good thing *someone* likes to play at religion—if it had been left up to the majority voices of Christendom to choose, this book of Esther—rich in satire, filled with burlesque, robust with court intrigue and bursting with a cast of wild characters—would have been relegated to a position of utter obscurity in the canon, if not removed from the Bible altogether. It was not until the latest revision of the *Common Lectionary*, in fact, that the book of Esther even showed up once on the three-year cycle of readings—for like the Song of Solomon, the canonical value of Esther has oft been discussed in a somewhat prim tone of disapproval. Here is a portion of the book's introduction in my study Bible:

> . . . the book has frequently been faulted for its moral tone. Not only are such basic Judaic values as kindness, mercy, and forgiveness lacking; but, as many Jews and Christians have lamented, the story evidences a vengeful, bloodthirsty, and chauvinistic spirit. Intrigue, deceit, and hatred abound, regardless of whether the spotlight is on Haman, Esther, Mordecai, or on their enemies. The Persian king is mentioned 190 times, but the God of Israel, not once.[14]

If you prefer your dose of Bible moralistic, straightforward, somber, and sacred—Esther is not your cup of tea. Neither, for that matter, is the teaching of Jesus recorded in this morning's text from the ninth chapter of the Gospel of Mark—a cutting, satiric partner to Esther's playful, yet deadly serious admonition that folks who want to make a difference in the world cannot afford to be too picky about ways and means while advancing the causes of God's forgotten peoples.

Esther is a story that comes to us from the time of the Jewish exile in Babylon. It was created by losers, for outsiders who had lost whatever prestige and economic power they had, who were abandoned by a theology of God's preferential option for his chosen, and who had been shaken to the core by social circumstances that seemed certain to destroy their faith and the fabric of their identity as a people. Because it comes from this place, this culture of desperation, it has little tolerance for the niceties of an Establishment Faith shaped by rules and regulations and watched over by a God who never alters his stern adherence to the system. The

---

14. *The New Oxford Annotated Bible*, p. 708.

people—and the God—of Esther (whether mentioned by name or not) have more pressing needs.

It reminds me of a story Gillian's dad told me when he phoned me on the eve of 1992's Hurricane Andrew. He had been on retreat at Ghost Ranch—a place so admirably remote that a television, telephone, or newspaper was hard to find. On the morning before Andrew struck, he was in a worship service at the retreat center, praying, along with others, for the needs and concerns of the world. Being a concerned citizen, and a new-ish pastor recently awakened to the social struggles of Miami's diverse community, Rick's prayer that morning was theologically, politically, and spiritually correct: he prayed for the racial strife in our city, for strength to do justice, for a new spirit of tolerance and so forth to come upon us. When the service was over, a stranger approached him and began to speak. *You're from Miami? You got more immediate concerns today than social harmony, buddy.* Rick, somewhat offended, said, *What do you mean? I think these problems are of utmost importance.* The man replied, *I guess you don't know it, but there's a Category 5 hurricane heading straight for Miami.*

When people's lives are at stake, other concerns—however just, right, or proper—must take a back seat. And that is what Esther proves by her creative interpretation of laws meant to destroy her people; in her wily, economical use of the poor resources available to her as an outsider, a woman, and an insignificant orphan; and in her triumphant seduction of the powers that be, the King Ahasuerus, into seeing the world through her eyes. Esther proves that there is a time and place to stop following the rules and start thinking for one's self. For when people's lives are in danger, unquestioning obedience is the wrong attitude. Indeed it is the sin of omission that opens the door to wholesale destruction: to neglect of the forgotten, to systematic extermination of the other; to a careless disregard of any value, any community, anyone who isn't part of us.

The book of Esther is subversive: not only does it insist that the outcast and the outsider are worth saving—it makes the astonishing claim that salvation itself *comes from* the outsiders. It avers that slavishly adhering to "the unchangeable law"—whether that law is Persia's, the Torah, or the Christian Scriptures—is a dangerous path to follow, one that leads to a soulless, heartless obedience to a set of rules and regulations at the expense of the safety, even the survival, of some of God's children—outsiders, minorities, the powerless, the poor. It says that, rather than being preoccupied with our powerlessness and our scarcity, we might do better to assess our gifts and graces—however little they may be valued in the grand scheme of things—and use them for good, however and whenever we can, for as long as we can. It promises that, if we will only try, the God who works unseen will not let our cries for justice, wholeness, and peace go unanswered.

Jesus himself in the ninth chapter of Mark says much the same thing—and surely practiced what he preached in his own life and ministry. When the disciples, still stinging from their failure to heal a child stricken with epilepsy, discover a stranger healing in Christ's name, they stop him. Proudly they tell the teacher: we saw some nobody healing in your name, and we stopped him, *because he wasn't one of us.* Jesus, who only just had finished reminding the disciples that if they could not love God and do God's work with childlike trust and humility, they were goners, just about loses it in his response to their self-righteous adherence to the rules. He tells them that if their correctness loses one soul for the kin-dom of God, they will surely pay with their own souls. He suggests that if their own correctness is standing in the way of loving and knowing God, they would do better to chew off their own leg than march, correctly dressed and impeccably credentialed, into the gates of orthodox hell. He reminds them that after all, everyone is going to suffer something, sometime—so why borrow trouble, or cause it for others? Use the trouble you have to season your compassion for another's sorrow . . . and be at peace.

We who want to serve the poor, the dispossessed, the outsider . . . who walk prayerfully along the margins of our increasingly narrow Presbyterian practice and polity, trying to find a canny and crafty way to celebrate our Christ's gospel of wild inclusivity—we would do well to listen to the voices in Esther, and celebrate the place—however small—organized religion has for scrappy, wily outsiders who do not have too much power, but use what they have for God with impressive imagination and verve. We might take heart when we listen to that other outsider, Jesus, as he walks toward his own salting with fire with head held high and a heart full of trust that *the least of these* will be the ones who will get it right for all of us, at last.

It takes a lot to be an Esther kind of community, a Jesus kind of church—but here we are, I hope, trying to do it. Standing this morning on the side of Esther, striving to be players for good in those small insignificant stories involving the kinds of people most folks would rather forget exist. Knowing that somehow, our life, and our salvation, depend on theirs. We are a small church in a big world, and it is all good. We will, like uncle Mordecai, find partners who are willing to assist us toward those goals. We are willing, like Esther, to use whatever resources we can find to help the homeless, feed the hungry, comfort those who suffer, extend the warmth of God's Light to people of all conditions and orientations, celebrate our unity with the communion of outsiders and outcasts. Like Esther and Jesus, we are not too picky about the way the job gets done. We can work with anyone who wants to work with us. We will set aside our doctrinal differences, and our theological imperatives if they get in the way of serving justice and love as Jesus commanded. We enter creatively into dialogue with our tradition and our polity, our law that cannot be changed, because we know that anything that cannot change will die. We want to live, and we can learn from this plucky little book buried in the back seat of the Bible that there is no skill, no idea, no quirk of personality, no circumstance so trivial or so undervalued that it cannot somehow be used for *tikkun olam*, for the healing of the world.

Let us pray,

> *God grant me the serenity to accept the things I cannot change, courage to change the things I can, and wisdom to know the difference; living one day at a time, enjoying one moment at a time, accepting hardship as a pathway to peace, taking, as Jesus did, this sinful world as it is, not as I would have it; trusting that you will make all things right if I surrender to your will, so that I may be reasonably happy in this life and supremely happy with you in the next.*[15] Amen.

ORDINARY TIME

Job 1:1—2:13

Losing God

This week, the oldest, hardest questions have been writ plain for us, and for anyone who has paused in the midst of the otherwise everyday to observe the bowed heads in their straw hats or clean lace caps, and the long, slow procession of black buggies carrying their unbearable load of small, simple pine boxes. If we have come from *going to and fro on the earth and from walking up and down on it,* as the opening of Job describes, surely we have considered God's servants the Amish this week, and considering,

---

15. Reinhold Niebuhr, 1941.

have many more hard questions about the ways of God in the world to add to our own, if that were possible.

So we take our places, while the curtain goes up again on this oldest of folk tales, among these most painful and unanswerable questions, on the book of Job.

About the author of the poem that constitutes the greatest part of the book of Job, we know next to nothing. As inspiration for his work, he drew upon a legend that was ancient generations before his telling of it; a folk story of uncertain provenance but universal application. It is the story of a righteous person from whom, for no reason, everything good has been taken away. It is a story about the deep and painful injustice of human life, seasoned by human suspicions about the injustice and the indifference of God and those who dwell with God in the realm of heaven. It is a story upon which people of faith can hang their most important questions, look for meaning in the midst of suffering, and begin to build a way of wisdom.

As we receive this poem, it is a work of many generations, a family conversation that seeks to make sense of how life is, especially in times of (undeserved) trouble. It is an ongoing conversation, into which we have been invited, to share what life is like for us when we are touched by pain; to listen to the experience of others; and to draw our own conclusions about how we will go on through it, and find God in the midst of it.

About this task, writer Stephen Mitchell has said *when we look at the world of the legendary Job with a probing, disinterestedly satanic eye, we notice that it is suffused with anxiety. Job is afraid of God, as well he might be. He avoids evil because he realizes the penalties.*[16] He is correct and "upright" in all his doings: even safeguarding the anticipated slips of his children through prayer and sacrifice lest any flaw put a crack in the walls of the shelter of righteousness he has erected to protect himself and those he loves. Nevertheless . . . he suspects, he fears, that he can never do enough to be utterly safe in a world that is unstable . . . and it turns out that he is right.

It does not take the power of evil, personified in a devil of fire surrounded by demons, to show Job, or to show us, that the world, even with God in the midst of it, is not a safe place. Indeed, in the Book of Job we would be missing the mark if we saw this character "Satan" as the personi-

---

16. Mitchell, *The Book of Job*, ix.

fication of evil. Rather, in the ancient world from which Job's story comes, as in the Jewish world of the poet-author, *ha satan* is merely the Adversary, one of any number of angelic beings whose job it was from time to time to block, obstruct, or challenge a human or divine activity. As Elaine Pagels points out in her book, *The Origin of Satan*, the presence of the Satan in Jewish stories, like the character of the "Trickster" in Navajo legend, helped explain unexpected reversals in fortune or unanticipated changes in direction. In the book of Numbers, when the prophet Baalam undertakes a wrong-headed journey against the purposes of God, it is the Satan who appears as an angel on the path to stop Balaam's donkey in its tracks.

In Job, it is *ha satan's* obligation to question the roots of fidelity in a man who has no real reason not to bless God, since his life has been experienced as unmitigated blessing. This is not the looming presence of evil: it is rather, the mythic articulation of a profound but very human question: *what will we do when trouble overcomes us? How will we handle our journey through suffering—with integrity?—in relationship with God and one another?—or by cursing God, and dying,* as Job's wife suggests he should do, when his wealth, his children, and his health have been taken away from him.

In the work I am privileged to do as a pastor, I hear this perspective addressed every time someone calls me to report an illness, a loss, or a personal catastrophe and says in some form or another *I want to say, "why me?" but I know that to spend time on that question is fruitless. I might better say, "why not me?" and then get on with the business of making my way through this hard time.*

The solutions we come up with—in restless hours of sleeplessness, in deeply wounded places of internal conversation, in privileged exchange among trusted friends, in prayer; may harm us or help us: we are trying, like Job, to become whole again when life has shattered us into pieces. Sometimes, we come to understand that we were not whole to begin with: that the work catastrophe has brought to us is a work we needed to be doing all along. The great rabbinic teacher Maimonides said about Job *he was a good man, but not a wise one.* Perhaps in the work of suffering, wisdom and wholeness can be built upon the foundation of goodness, and the person who comes to him or herself after suffering may be stronger for it; but there is a long journey to be taken, and much work to do before we can look back at what we might have learned, how we may have grown.

The poet of the Book of Job places in the mouths of Job's family and friends any number of "solutions" to Job's condition. Job's wife says, *give up your faith, curse God and quit.* Job's friends, after working through what might have been the better part of love by sitting in silence with the suffering Job for a week, find that they cannot resist the urge to fix what has been broken in Job's (not to mention their own) naïve and safe worldview. They voice harsh, simplistic answers—answers we have all heard before, and sometimes even spoken. Sometimes even a bad answer seems better than silence when the world and our place in it have been turned upside down.

Many of these "bad" solutions, spoken by Job's good friends Bildad, Eliphaz, and Zophar, are familiar, and arise from familiar sources. They are the voices of moral certainty in a morally uncertain world. They tell us that if God is good, then evil must only befall those who have failed in goodness or fallen from the morally correct life. They suggest that this is how the system of divine reward and punishment plays out: and they order us to examine ourselves, confess our sin, and begin to appreciate the justice of what is happening to us, even if we do not understand it. Lest we judge them too harshly for their harsh solutions to their friend's pain, let us remember that they, too, are suffering and afraid. They know that the next time, it might be one of them. Only by holding to their small vision of a predictable world of right and wrong can they keep a much needed distance between themselves and their destroyed friend. Only by pretending that it cannot happen to them (unless they should happen to sin) can they bear to remain with Job in his unanswerable pain. They want an answer, a way out, as much for themselves as for their friend. And the voice of Job's wife, which is the only other path they can imagine, is impossible: to admit that the world and its ways are absurd, to give up and renounce belief in the goodness of God, and, stripped of even that small moral core, to utterly collapse, relinquish their humanity, and die.

The path upon which Job will walk involves anger, bargaining, grief, and denial—all the stages of grief we must endure before finding our way to acceptance. It is a work that takes all his time, his energy, and his resources. In this work, there is not room for much else. Martin Buber, the post-Holocaust philosopher and writer relates this story: *One of the followers of the Rabbi of Kobryn was very poor. He complained to the rabbi about his straits, which, as he said, put him off his studies and made him unable to pray. The rabbi told him: "in these times, the greatest piety, which supersedes study and prayer, is to accept the world as it is."*

There are no good answers here, even among beloved friends. There is only silence, the prayer-speech of anger, grief, and lament, and the fragile beginnings of a new conversation, rooted in utter honesty and naked in need. It is a conversation whose ending we cannot imagine, but without which we cannot hope to survive, or thrive.

It is our conversation, our chance, and our responsibility: no one else's.

One of the great ancient Hasidic masters, Rabbi Barukh of Medzebozh put it this way: *I know there are questions that have no answers; there is a suffering that has no name; there is injustice in God's creation;—and there are reasons enough for man to explode with rage. I know there are reasons for you to be angry. Good. Let us be angry. Together.*[17]

Amen.

ORDINARY TIME

Psalm 131   Job 38

Dancing With Chaos

Who is this who darkens counsel without knowledge?

Words get in the way.

Job learned this the hard way—first, by listening and then by speaking.

Failing at both, Job discovered that there really is nothing anyone can say in the face of loss. No case to be made, no explanation good enough, no words of comfort adroit enough. In the end, however well meant, however eloquently expressed, however hard and long we try to get it right—words get in the way, for what we need in the end is not to comprehend what has happened to us, but rather, to know that we are in God.

I went to Texas last week because my brother Scot was killed in a car accident last Saturday morning. When it happened, my parents were out of town, and so I was the one to tell them that their only son was dead. There are no words to break such news. Anyone who has ever had to do it, or to hear it, knows this. One asks for details, for repetition; one tells the story over and over again until it sounds like a recitation of Scripture—but

---

17. Wiesel, *Four Hasidic Masters and Their Struggle Against Melancholy*, 60.

the words fall like water around you, growing deeper and darker until you think you might drown if you cannot somehow reach the surface and breathe fresh air.

The other words that kept repeating themselves in my mind during this past week were Job's, from chapter 23, his words of despair and inadequacy as he acknowledged at last that there was no comfort to be found in the explanation of friends or in his own poignant demands for justification . . . because while he and his friends thought they wanted answers, what they really wanted was something else altogether.

Job needed God, and all the words in the world could not bring him into that Presence for which he yearned:

> *If I go East—He is not there; West—I still do not perceive Him;*
> *North—since He is concealed, I do not behold Him;*
> *South—He is hidden, and I cannot see Him.*[18]

Faced with the unanswerable, we make the mistake of believing that God is on the other side of the question *why*. And we look for God there, in proposals of cause and effect, in condolences and constructions of belief . . . we are looking for a God of answers, but we will not find him. But that there is no God of answers does not mean there is no God:

> *But He knows the way I take; And I am not cut off*
> *by the darkness;*
> *He has concealed the thick gloom from me.*[19]

I am not cut off by the darkness. It is perhaps the most powerful affirmation of faith in the bible. Like the words of the distraught father of the epileptic boy in the gospel of Mark, when Jesus asked him if he believed God could heal his son, it is an affirmation that closes one door and opens another. *Lord, I believe, help my unbelief.* Making such an affirmation, we close the door on the god of certainties, the god of easy answers and quick comfort, and we open the door to a God we have not yet come to know, before whom we tremble, God who stands in the thick darkness before us, holding out a hand.

When we open that door, as Job did, God answers out of the whirlwind, with words that do not explain and cannot yet comfort; words of power and compassion and truth:

---

18. Job 23:8–9, *TANAKH—The Holy Scriptures*.
19. Job 23:17, *TANAKH—The Holy Scriptures*.

The Greening of the Gospel

Who is this who darkens counsel speaking without knowledge? Gird up your loins like a man, because I'm asking the questions now.[20]

What follows here in the book of Job for four long chapters in a section quaintly titled "God Answers Job" seems to be an extended poetic treatment, a theme-and-variation on a single question: *Just who in hell do you think you are?*

Who do you think you are? Did you create heaven and earth? Do you cause the rain to fall, or the sun to shine? Can you find your way to Light, or open the gates of hell? Is it by your explanations, your strength, your goodness that the seasons follow upon one another and the birds and fish and animals multiply after their kind? And if it were and if you could, would it answer the pain you are feeling now? *Who do you think you are?*

It seems harsh, it seems unnecessarily cruel, almost, to point out how helpless, how limited we are when we are already so raw with that knowledge, in the face of our suffering and loss. You hear people say it all the time, indeed, I heard myself say it this past week: *let his wife decide, she needs to have some sense of control, when she has lost so much*—as if choosing a piece of music for the funeral could stop the train of chaos that is her life for this little while. We have no control, we never did: control is an illusion, and a bad one at that. I learned that this week as well, as my family and their pastor turned to me to make the service, speak the words, do the work for which I have been trained ... and not one thing I said or did made any difference at all to the fact that my brother is gone, and I cannot bring him back, and there is no way past the loss except to go through it.

God's word, God's *answer* to Job is the best of a bad job: to let us know that we are not responsible to make everything better, it is not our fault nor our privilege to fix it; and if we think any differently, we have strayed from the path of wisdom. *Who the hell do you think you are?* It is the best of questions, and it is no accident that in the book of Job, it is repeated twice by God and echoed at the very end by Job himself. For what is hell, except the place where we believe we act with utter autonomy, free from God and free from anyone else? Where our answers alone echo in our own head, our ideas form the heavens and the earth, and all that is not of *me* is nothing. What is hell, if not the place of complete isolation where we declare *I am God, I myself am all the god I need*?

20. Job 38:1, Ibid.

This is the time and place, the season of loss in which we can lose our fantasies about our own omnipotence, lay down the burden of responsibility for the bad things that happen in this world of God's making, offer up our weariness into the hands and the arms of another. Someone else can say the words of the creed we do not at this moment believe for ourselves. Another's voice can sustain the melody of our broken song; someone else's back can bear the load, someone's hands slip quietly into our own, Someone's arms enfold us.

We are not alone, we are with God, and we belong to each other.

And when God describes for Job the world that *God* has made, the world that *God* has made free—it is not God's power and omnipotence that is being described, but rather God's own sense of wonder at what is unfolding, both the bad and the good of it; God's sense of companionship with us as creation continues to unfold, in us and in God's own heart. God is dancing with chaos, as we are—God has being doing it since the day of creation; but *even in the darkness, we are not cut off, and God has hidden the deepest gloom from us.* This is the oldest of words, and the best: it is Christ on the cross, crying with one breath *my god, my God, why have you forsaken me?* and then with the next, *father, into your hands I commend my spirit.*

We are doing God's work here: and we are not alone.

ALL SAINTS DAY

Psalm 46   Joshua 3:14-17   Revelation 21:1-4

Cry Me a River ...

My grandfather lost his wife, my cookie-baking, vegetable-canning Canadian grandmother Loma, when I was in the sixth grade, and she was in her early sixties. There was a series of late-night, solemn phone calls conducted in stark whispers, a hurried trip to Wisconsin for my father, and, when he returned, a ring that had belonged to my Grandma now belonged to me. Death was not an appropriate subject for children; and so, to all intents and purposes, it did not happen. The next summer, my grandfather came to Oklahoma to visit us, alone ... and though I watched him carefully for two weeks, I detected no evidence that loss, or grief had changed him ... I was both frightened, and relieved. On the day he left to return home, we all piled into the car to ride to the airport. Blocks away from his departure, I glanced over at him, sitting behind my father, looking out the backseat window. Though his face was still, his eyes were glimmering, and as I watched furtively, a single tear trembled on the edge of his lid, spilled over, and made its slow, lonely way down the side of his face, until at last it was evaporated by the hot, dry wind blowing through our car. We did not speak of it.

I think it is no accident that Protestants, constitutionally edgy about excesses of emotion, replaced the Sunday observation of All Saints Day with the more bracing *Reformation Sunday* . . . stoic, resolute, intellectual, historical. While other Christians offer themselves up to the idea that there is a world of the spirit, a world of loss and intercession, a reservoir of aching need and shimmering hope toward which we earth-bound ones yearn with passionate prayer; Protestant and Reformed Christians gird up their loins, think about all the tasks yet to be done (*reformed . . . and always reforming*) and celebrate our rectitude and our work ethic. The observance of All Saints' we leave to the accidents of the calendar and the safety of a weekday, where, God knows, none of us would ever take enough time off from work to think about our losses, our sorrows, our grief.

We model this rectitude culturally by encouraging folks to "get on with living" mere days after the death of a loved one. We praise bereaved spouses who get back to work, back to business quickly, suffering no apparent ill from their loss. We mock politicians whose passion for justice or whose tender awareness of the fragility of life renders them vulnerable to public displays of emotion . . . in all walks of life, we are deeply resistant to acknowledging our vulnerability, our lack of control over the deep forces of life and death. We do not want to weep.

But there is still weeping to be done . . . weeping that cannot be hidden behind a wall of placid acceptance; weeping that should not be inappropriately translated into political fervor, weeping that does not show our weakness, but rather reveals our strength, our knowledge of the way things *should* be, but aren't, weeping that unleashes our hope for a better future. And we must not permit *this* weeping to pass unseen, or unheard.

In a way, All Saints is about the acknowledgement of human grief—in all its dimensions—and about the healing of it. In the pagan and Celtic traditions that caused the celebration of All Saints to exist, and to be located on November 1 (just after All Hallows Eve and before All Souls' Day, November 2) it was intended that the work of grieving and letting go should be taken seriously. Hallows Eve was a time to recognize those who had been lost, and to free the living from bondage to the dead——a bondage that could be haunting, draining, even frightening to those whose lives remained centered in the earth. The dead were fed, blessed, made free to leave—the living were protected from meddling (and from an inappropriate ongoing influence). In the Mexican tradition of *Dia de los Muertos*, the Day of the Dead, offerings of food, flowers and small mementos are brought in procession to the cemeteries where families set a picnic among the gravestones, and honor those they have lost. Jewish families sit *shiva* for seven days, praying and telling stories, and mourn for a full year, ending their grieving at the *yartzeit*, the anniversary, with the placing of the headstone. Grief and loss are powerful forces in us: too important to treat with covert haste. By taking our weeping seriously, we acknowledge the bittersweet gift of life, and we claim that both in life and death, God will give us comfort, and make us whole. God will wipe away every tear from their eyes, and sorrow and sighing shall flee away.

The Bible is full of weeping . . . weeping that begins in the waters of chaos that the ancients feared, and prayed that God would order and transform. Weeping that flooded Noah's world of wickedness and depravity, destroying life, and with it, the illusion that human ingenuity could master the unpredictability of divine whimsy, or fate. Weeping that acknowledged the wrongness of a mother's inability to protect the life of her child, weeping that sent fleeing slaves into the terror of the Red Sea and flooded over their enemies with waters that roared and raged. The Bible is full of weeping that feeds evil's hunger for human pain, that expresses the prophets' sorrow at justice unfulfilled, that speaks to a people's deep yearning for comfort, for power, for peace, that cries for the dam of God's mercy and the Spirit's kindness to channel an ocean of human suffering into a manageable river, a river that does not destroy us, but instead nourishes our community, our people, our lives.

It is not that we do not need to cry: it is that we need to cry differently.

We do not weep as those who are without hope. This is what the Apostle Paul said, and I take him to mean that the weeping of people of faith should not serve to fill the ocean of hopelessness and chaos, but should instead fuel the wellspring of mercy. We do not weep as those who are without hope: so we do weep like Hagar, who cried to a god who alone could see her, and for the wrongness of the abandonment of her son. We weep for the victims of snipers, for the death of a friend, for a bomb exploding in the midst of a busy marketplace, for Haitian refugees who braved the chaos of the sea only to huddle, unwelcomed on a causeway at the mouth of the river. We do weep like the prophets, for a world numb and indifferent to human suffering, for the passion to *let justice roll down like waters, and righteousness like an ever-flowing stream.*

It is the love of God around us and the passion of God within us that invites us to *cry me a river*: a river of mercy, a river of life . . . and to make of our weeping, something good, something strong, something powerful. When the Israelites fled Egypt and wandered in the wilderness, they came at last through their season of terror and weeping to the River Jordan. Into that River the priests and the hopeful, hapless community of Israel waded by their own free choice, fleeing no one, walking gladly toward their promise of a future of goodness, plenty, a land of "milk and honey." They had cried a river and fled a raging sea—and here, in the midst of Jordan, with the glory of God in the ark of the covenant at last their constant companion, they entered the land of promise, centered in the presence of God, sure of a future. The Psalm reminds us: *There is a river whose streams make glad the city of God* . . . and when God shall wipe away every tear, the book of Revelation tells us, *the sea will be no more.* The oceans of useless pain and evil's suffering will be drained once and for all, and our tears channeled into the river of life. Our crying, our mourning, our relentless exposure to human suffering will fuel in us in us a passionate belief in the God who said, *the sea will be no more.* That is where our weeping must lead us: away from the sea, and on to the River. *Blessed are they that mourn* . . . said Jesus, *for they shall be comforted.*

Let our sorrow fuel a river full of healing intention, a nourishing, cleansing shower of justice, a rain of mercy, a fountain of love. Let us turn our mourning into dancing: not just because our tears are played out, but because our tears are the waters that slake our thirst for the presence of God in the world, and for the river of life, our source and our future.

> *Like a river glorious, is God's perfect peace*
> *Over all victorious in its bright increase.*
> *Perfect, yet it floweth fuller every day*
> *Perfect yet it groweth deeper all the way.*
> *Stayed upon Jehovah hearts are fully blest;*
> *Finding as He promised, perfect peace and rest.*[21]

---

21. "Like a River Glorious" by Frances R. Havergal, in *Soul-Stirring Songs & Hymns*, 98.

Tuning My Heart

THE REIGN OF CHRIST OR CHRIST THE KING

John 18:33–37   *Revelation 1:4b–8*   *2 Samuel 23:1–7*

An Embarrassing Anachronism

A few days after the 2000 presidential election, I received the following notice from one of our proper British congregants:

> *Notice of Revocation of Independence*
>
> *To the citizens of the United States of America: In light of your failure to elect anybody as President of the USA and thus to govern yourselves and, by extension, the free world, we hereby give notice of the revocation of your independence, effective today. Her Sovereign Majesty Queen Elizabeth II will resume monarchial duties over all states, commonwealths and other territories except Utah, which she does not fancy. Tax collectors from Her Majesty's Government will be with you shortly to ensure the acquisition of all revenues due (back dated to 1776). Thank you for your cooperation, and have a nice day.*

After three weeks of endless, mind-numbing post-election "news" coverage, and with only a slim hope of an end in sight, the Queen's looking better and better . . .

A monarch is, after all, in the classical sense, an ultimate solution to the messy problems of self-government. A clear answer to the ambiguities, the sloppiness, the lack of clarity and purpose that seems to afflict our body politic—and will continue to afflict it, I am convinced, even after this election is finally decided. Oh, for a king to rule justly, to wear the mantle of justice nobly, to assume the divine right, to assure the people that God's chosen vessel has things firmly in hand and all will be well: *ah, wouldn't it be loverly?*

Thus we come to the final Sunday of the church year, the conclusion of the story which began with Advent, the season of anticipation of the coming of Jesus: the Sunday called *Christ the King*. Christ the *King?* Oh, *we've just done away with* that, averred a most progressive clergy friend of mine when we spoke on the phone yesterday, *I just can't believe in it anymore.* My friend is not alone, I think: indeed, the Church itself, sensing this discomfort with the notion of absolute power that rides piggyback on the shoulders of the word "King," has with immense sensitivity and political correctness renamed this Sunday *The Reign of Christ*. Which, I guess, is supposed to make us look less supremacist when we celebrate what is, baldly put, a Sunday designed to celebrate the eventual triumph of the Christian faith over the entire world. A quick survey of the hymns penned for this illustrious occasion remind us what it is still, really, all about:

> *Crown Him with many crowns, the Lamb upon his throne: hark, how the heavenly anthem drowns all music but its own. All hail the power of Jesus' name, let angels prostrate fall. Bring forth the royal diadem, and crown him Lord of All. Jesus shall reign where'er the sun does its successive journeys run. Hail to the Lord's anointed. Rejoice, the Lord is king.*

Christ the King? The Reign of Christ? By any other name, it still says this: we, no less than Al Gore or George W. Bush, do not want to end up losers, footnotes in a history book, a forgotten dream, crumbling into dust and ruins.

Christ the King. I get why my friend wants to pretend it does not exist . . . but the fact is, it does. Like the elephant in the living room we politely ignore, the idea of Christ the King has dominated the church's silent reveries, sustained its will in times of oppression, undergirded its self-justification in countless wars of religion—and in the end, shaped and distorted our believing and the practice of our faith in ways we can only hope to address if we begin to admit how much we really *want* to be God's winners.

Each year, the scripture texts dished up for the Sunday of Christ the King trot out a smorgasbord of images designed to remind the church that, although the church of Jesus may be weak now, someday, we will get ours, and everybody will see things our way. Readings from the Hebrew Scriptures caress the royal ideology of the dynasty of David: the dream that it was God, not human beings, who selected the boy David, put him on the throne, and perpetuated the dynasty founded in his blood. Pairing these texts with scriptures from the gospels, we are meant to understand that the reign of the risen Christ is the true successor to David's divinely mandated rule. We are intended to see that although Jesus himself said *my kingdom is not of this world,* (and refused to entertain the notion that he was in any way to be considered a king) that God himself will, in the end, subject everything and everyone in the world to the Lordship of this long-dead Palestinian Jewish teacher whom we call Jesus the Christ.

From such theologies—unexamined and unremarked—come the questions I still receive from every confirmation class, even in this pluralistic, post-Christian place and time: *will people who have never heard of Christ still go to hell? Are Jews going to get to heaven? What about Buddhists? Muslims? Pagans? Does God love them? Or just us?*

From such theologies comes the Holocaust. The bitter, endless warring of the Balkans. The smug assurances that Christmas, Easter, even Sunday—ought to be protected holidays, sacrosanct, because they are *our* holy days.

We want to believe about our faith, about our lives, about our people—shapes the way we look at others, and the way we live in the world. A man I respected as a great amateur historian specializing in the period of the United States' westward expansion shocked me one day with his impassioned defense of Manifest Destiny and the American Way of Life which, as he said, made our decimation of the Native American population of this country justifiable: *we offered them a better way of life, and they refused to accept it.*

Christ the King.

Our vision of ourselves—however idealized—determines our relationships, and controls what we do, what we see, and how much we are able to change and grow. If we drink or use drugs or eat abusively, but consider ourselves merely "social" users, occasional bingers—we cannot hope to change our behavior. If our final word about who we are is *I am a nice guy, I am a wonderful human being,* nothing will intrude upon our vision. It will take more than a little spousal battering, a tiny cheat on our income tax, or an insensitivity to anyone weaker, alien, different—to stand in the way of our self-congratulation. Both Al Gore and George Bush believed they won that election: and their belief controls the actions in which both camps are currently engaged. Christ the King.

How many of you have been to a funeral where the officiating clergy and eulogists described a person so perfect, so astounding in every way that the image being created of the dearly departed bore no resemblance whatsoever to the living, breathing, deeply flawed human being whose life you had come to honor? Hearing such a eulogy, did you feel surprised? Cheated of your more negative memories? Robbed of the chance to grieve what had been left unfinished, unsaid, and imperfect, and feeling slightly guilty that your own view was so, well, ambivalent? Christ the

The Greening of the Gospel

King thinking wants us to practice a faith that is wrapped up, finished, triumphant—if not now, then, well, someday soon, darn it.

Christ the King thinking does not want us to remember that Jesus died, a criminal on a Roman cross, and his followers all ran away and hid, because they were terrified. Christ the King thinking does not want us to look too closely at the Jesus who made a vocation of his association with losers, whores, dishonest professionals, invisible people and failures, and who demanded that his followers do the same. Christ the King thinking would have us believe that a little sacrifice, a tiny bit of time in the trenches, a nod and a wink at the cross, will entitle us to glory evermore in the sweet by-and-by. Would have us believe that it will all turn out for our side in the end . . . when we have no reason, really, to believe that that is the way God will write it. Christ the King *presumes* the triumphant ending of a story that we have scarcely begun, ourselves, to write with our hearts and our lives. We need to remember the Sunday of Christ the King, if only to admit to ourselves once in a while, that we are ever prone to want our ends neatly tied up, our answers firmly in place, and the successful end of the story understood before we undertake to write it with our lives.

It is Christ the King. How many assumptions does our faith in the stories of Jesus cause us to make about the way things will all come out, in the end? How many opportunities are we missing, hurtling past chances with our eyes firmly fixed on a predetermined, glorious destination? How much are we willing to lose of ourselves, in our relationships, by relying on what we *know* to be true about them, about us, using all our energy to ignore or explain away evidence that does not support our presumed verdict?

How much more satisfying, in the end, to view our lives as an Advent—a time of coming and becoming—in which, in company with the humble mystery that was Jesus of Nazareth, we walk a path toward God as blank slates upon which the Spirit of God, and we, God's children, might write anything whatsoever. Amen.

Bibliography

Branch, Taylor. Parting the Waters: *America in the King Years, 1954–1963.* New York: Simon and Schuster, 1994.

Brueggemann, Walter. *Genesis. Interpretation, a Bible Commentary for Teaching and Preaching.* Louisville, KY: John Knox, 1987.

———. *First and Second Samuel. Interpretation, a Bible Commentary for Teaching and Preaching.* Louisville, KY: John Knox, 1990.

Buber, Martin. *Tales of the Hasidim: The Early Masters.* Translated by Olga Marx. New York: Schocken, 1947.

———. *Tales of the Hasidim: The Later Masters.* Translated by Olga Marx. New York: Schocken, 1948.

Dillard, Annie. "Holy the Firm." In *The Annie Dillard Reader.* New York: HarperCollins, 1994.

Goldsmith, Martin. *The Inextinguishable Symphony*, New York: Wiley, 2000.

Isasi-Díaz, Ada María. Mujerista Theology: *A Theology for the Twenty-first Century.* Maryknoll, NY: Orbis, 1996.

Lowry, James S. "Deep Dawn." *Journal for Preachers* 28 No. 3 (2004).

Lamott, Anne. *Plan B: Further Thoughts on Faith.* New York: Riverhead, 2005.

Lathem, Edward Connery, ed. *The Poetry of Robert Frost.* New York: Holt, Rinehart and Winston, 1969.

Lewis, C. S. *Till We Have Faces, A Myth Retold.* Grand Rapids, MI: Eerdmans, 1956.

Minear, P. S. "Babylon." In *The Interpreter's Dictionary of the Bible, A–D,* edited by George Arthur Buttrick, 334–38. Nashville: Abingdon, 1962.

Mitchell, Stephen. *The Book of Job.* New York: HarperPerennial, 1992.

Moore, James W, *And the Angels Wept: from the Pulpits of Oklahoma City After the Bombing,* St. Louis: Chalice, 1995.

Peterson, Eugene H. *The Message: The Bible in Contemporary Language.* Colorado Springs: NavPress, 2002.

Rice, John R., and Joy Rice Martin. *Soul-Stirring Songs & Hymns.* Murfreesboro, TN: Sword of the Lord, 1972.

Sabin, Marie Noonan. *Reopening the Word: Reading Mark as Theology in the Context of Early Judaism.* New York: Oxford University Press, 2002.

Taylor, Barbara Brown. *God in Pain: Teaching Sermons on Suffering.* Edited by Ronald J. Allen. Nashville, TN: Abingdon, 1998.

Tirabassi, Maren C. and Kathy Wonson Eddy, eds. *Gifts of Many Cultures.* Cleveland, Ohio: United Church Press, 1995.

Wiesel, Elie. *Four Hasidic Masters and Their Struggle Against Melancholy.* Notre Dame: University of Notre Dame Press, 1978.

www.ingramcontent.com/pod-product-compliance
Lightning Source LLC
Chambersburg PA
CBHW050808160426
43192CB00010B/1681